Leaders of the Colonial Era

William Bradford

Leaders of the Colonial Era

Lord Baltimore

Benjamin Banneker

William Bradford

Benjamin Franklin

Anne Hutchinson

Cotton Mather

William Penn

John Smith

Miles Standish

Peter Stuyvesant

Leaders of the Colonial Era

William Bradford

Heather Lehr Wagner

CHELSEA HOUSE
PUBLISHERS

An imprint of Infobase Publishing

WILLIAM BRADFORD

Chelsea House
An imprint of Infobase Publishing
132 West 31st Street
New York, NY 10001

Library of Congress Cataloging-in-Publication Data
Wagner, Heather Lehr.
  William Bradford / Heather Lehr Wagner.
    p. cm. — (Leaders of the colonial era)
  Includes bibliographical references and index.
  ISBN 978-1-60413-743-9 (hardcover)
  1. Bradford, William, 1590–1657—Juvenile literature. 2. Pilgrims (New Plymouth Colony)—Biography—Juvenile literature. 3. Governors—Massachusetts—Biography—Juvenile literature. 4. Massachusetts—History—New Plymouth, 1620–1691—Juvenile literature. 5. Plymouth (Mass.)—Biography—Juvenile literature. I. Title. II. Series.
  F68.B8235W54 2010
  974.4'02092—dc22
  [B]   2010010335

You can find Chelsea House on the World Wide Web at
http://www.chelseahouse.com

Text design by Kerry Casey
Cover design by Keith Trego
Composition by EJB Publishing Services
Cover printed by Bang Printing, Brainerd, Minn.
Book printed and bound by Bang Printing, Brainerd, Minn.
Date printed: November 2010
Printed in the United States of America

10 9 8 7 6 5 4 3 2 1

This book is printed on acid-free paper.

All links and Web addresses were checked and verified to be correct at the time of publication. Because of the dynamic nature of the Web, some addresses and links may have changed since publication and may no longer be valid.

Contents

1

On Board the *Mayflower*

William Bradford stood on the deck of the *Mayflower* and gazed across the water at the land that was to become his new home. It was November 9, 1620, and the 31-year-old Bradford had spent the past 65 days traveling across the Atlantic Ocean from Plymouth, England. Bradford knew little about the strange new world that lay before him. But as he looked at the cliffs of sand that stretched out in front of tree-covered hills, he and the other passengers "were not a little joyful," he wrote in his journal, later published as *Of Plymouth Plantation*.

Many of those on board the *Mayflower*, like Bradford, had traveled to this new land in search of a place where they could freely worship while establishing an English colony. France, Holland, and Spain funded expeditions to the New World and built settlements there. England's efforts had been less successful—a colony in Maine had failed and the colony in Jamestown, Virginia, had not proved as financially rewarding as its investors had hoped.

Bradford and other members of his church were known as Separatists. They had separated from the official Church of England (an act that could mean imprisonment) and fled to Holland, where they set up a church community and lived for nearly 12 years. It was a difficult life. Bradford and many of the other refugees who had farmed family plots in England were forced to seek work in Holland's textile businesses. Bradford had become a corduroy worker.

But after 12 years, the members of Bradford's congregation no longer felt welcome in Holland. They were increasingly harassed by the Dutch government for their religious beliefs. Their children were losing touch with their English roots and, in some cases, rejecting their religious practices. They decided to seek a patent from the Virginia Company, which would allow them to attempt to found a colony in five to seven years. If the attempt was successful, they could then apply for a new patent granting permanent rights to the land.

"The place they fixed their thoughts upon was somewhere in those vast and unpeopled countries of America," Bradford wrote, "which were fruitful and fit for habitation." Bradford and his wife, Dorothy, were among the members of the congregation who chose to make the journey and help build the colony. Fearing the unknown, they decided to leave their three-year-old son, John, behind with relatives.

The plans for the trip were hampered by delays and problems. Originally, 125 members of Bradford's church had volunteered to make the journey. Others agreed to follow once the colony was established. The original group planned to sail on two ships. The smaller, quicker ship, the *Speedwell*, left the Dutch port of Delfshaven in July 1620 bound for Southampton in England. There it would meet up with a larger British ship and together they would cross the Atlantic.

This larger ship was the *Mayflower*. The plan was for the two ships to make the journey across the Atlantic Ocean in the summer. But after setting sail from Southampton the *Speedwell* began to leak. Both ships were forced to change direction and sail to Dartmouth, 75 miles (120.7 kilometers) west of Southampton along the English coast, where they waited while the *Speedwell* underwent repair. By the time the repairs were completed the wind had changed and they were stuck in Dartmouth for several weeks. The food supplies they had carefully stored for the journey began to dwindle, and some passengers openly worried whether or not they would have enough to last the trip. Fearing that they would abandon the ship—and the journey—the captain refused to allow them to disembark. Finally, the wind picked up and they were able to sail out of the harbor.

The *Speedwell* began to leak again when they were more than 200 miles (321.8 km) beyond the southwestern tip of England. They turned back and headed for Plymouth, 50 miles (80.5 km) west of Dartmouth. It was now painfully clear that the *Speedwell* could not be trusted to make the journey across the Atlantic. Bradford and his fellow passengers had planned to keep the *Speedwell* for at least a year after reaching America. The plan was to use it for fishing and transportation along the coast. Its loss was a bitter blow.

In addition, they now needed to decide who would continue on the journey aboard the *Mayflower* and who would remain behind. Several chose to give up their places and remain in England. The journey seemed ill-fated, and the month of delays had cost them a significant portion of their supplies. They had spent several weeks on board a ship and still had not crossed the Atlantic.

In the end, Bradford and his wife were among only 50 members of the congregation who decided to continue on the journey. Half of the *Mayflower*'s passengers were not members of their church, but instead were what Bradford called "Strangers," people traveling to America for reasons other than religious beliefs. Several had made the

The Pilgrims boarded the *Speedwell* and departed Delfshaven in search of religious freedom in the New World. The leaky ship would never make it to America, however.

journey to America before. A total of 102 passengers were crowded into a space intended to accommodate no more than 90. Finally, on September 6, 1620, the *Mayflower* left Plymouth.

SIXTY-FIVE DAYS

The *Mayflower* was about 100 feet (30.5 meters) long and 25 feet (7.6 m) wide, with six large sails powering the ship. During rough weather, the sails were drawn in to prevent the winds from blowing the ship too far off course. In his book, *Mayflower*, Nathaniel Philbrick wrote that the ship averaged a speed of only two miles (3.21 km) an hour during the crossing.

Bradford and the other 101 passengers spent most of the 65 days in an area referred to as between, or 'tween, decks. This was a dark space less than 5 feet (1.5 m) high and about 75 feet (22.9 m) long. The only privacy came from makeshift, thin "walls" the passengers created around themselves, often made of their possessions (chests of clothing, chairs, and rugs). When the weather was rough, the passengers and their possessions were tossed about, resulting in bruises and injuries. Chamber pots served as toilets.

Below the 'tween decks was the hold, where most of the passengers' possessions were stored, as well as the food supplies for the journey. Ships at the time were measured by how many "tuns" or barrels of wine they could carry. Because the *Mayflower* could carry 180 barrels of wine, it was one of the largest merchant vessels of its time. In addition to wine, the *Mayflower*'s hold contained beer, water (although water was considered unsafe to drink in the seventeenth century), sugar, spices, crackers, rice, oatmeal, cheese, furniture, and tools. Meals were prepared in the forecastle, at the front of the ship, and generally consisted of very simple food designed to last without refrigeration during the long journey. Typical foods included oatmeal, peas, heavily salted pork (similar to bacon), dried fish, beans, and cheese.

The ship was steered below deck, where the helmsman moved the rudder in response to instructions shouted to him by someone standing on an upper deck. A course was charted based on often-faulty maps and using the position of stars and the horizon to estimate a ship's north-south direction.

As they sailed across the 3,000 miles (4,828 km) separating England from the New World, the weather was often rough, and many of the passengers became seasick. Bradford wrote in his journal of a sailor who spent much of the early part of the journey cursing at the passengers and mocking those who were ill, telling them "that he hoped to help throw half of them overboard before they came to their journey's end." Bradford happily notes that "it pleased God, before they came half seas over, to smite the young man with a grievous disease, of which he died in a desperate manner, and so was himself the first to be thrown overboard."

About halfway across the Atlantic a strong wave crashed across the deck, cracking one of the masts and causing the master (as the ship's captain was called) to consider turning back to England. But the mast was repaired using a tool brought by the colonists to build homes.

Supplies dwindled. They ran out of firewood and then faced shortages of beer, which they considered a much safer beverage than water.

As Nathaniel Philbrick notes in *Mayflower*, this group of colonists was quite different from others that had traveled to the New World. The colony of Jamestown in Virginia had been founded by noblemen and craftsmen with their servants. Most early colonists were men whose motives were largely profit. But most of those aboard the *Mayflower* were families, half of whom were making the difficult voyage seeking a place where they could freely practice their faith. Of the 102 passengers, 69 were adults, most of whom were in their thirties. There were 14 passengers between the ages of 13 and 18, and 19 children who were 12 years old or younger. Two baby boys were born during the journey.

The colonists had been given a patent to legally settle a stretch of land near the mouth of the Hudson River, in what is now the state of New York. But the rough winds had blown the *Mayflower* 220 miles (354 km) north of their destination. When they finally saw land on November 9, it was a stretch of land known even then as Cape Cod. The name had come from the schools of cod that swam along the shore. Fishing ships from England, Holland, and France sailed along the coast to gather up the rich harvest. A colony based in Cape Cod could benefit from the fishing trade, but Bradford and the other colonists did not have the legal right to settle there.

The master of the *Mayflower*, Christopher Jones, was more concerned by the sickness breaking out among his passengers than by delivering them to their preferred destination. He attempted to sail south, toward the Hudson, but the wind, shifting tides, and uncertainties about the hazards that lay along the shoreline quickly persuaded him to change his mind. By the end of the day he had decided instead to sail around the tip of Cape Cod to "New England," the relatively new name given to what we now know as the states of Massachusetts, Connecticut, Rhode Island, Maine, New Hampshire, and Vermont.

NEW DESTINATION

The news that the *Mayflower* was landing more than 200 miles (321.8 km) north of the Hudson River sparked conflict among the passengers. Many began loudly declaring that they would set out on their own as soon as they reached shore, since the terms that would have governed an English colony along the Hudson had no bearing in this unplanned destination. But it was clear that the settlement could only survive if all agreed to work together and respect certain basic rules and laws.

Over the course of the next day, as the *Mayflower* headed for the tip of Cape Cod, the passengers ironed out the agreement that would become the Mayflower Compact. The document simply and clearly stated that those who signed it had made this journey "to plant the first colony in the northern parts of Virginia" (at that time the eastern coast of America was broadly divided between what was known as "Virginia" and "New England"). They agreed to submit to any "just and equal laws" that were thought necessary "for the general good of the colony."

The *Mayflower*'s male passengers signed the Mayflower Compact as a pledge to abide by the colony's laws.

The colonists chose John Carver, one of the organizers of the voyage, to serve as their governor. Carver was a wealthy, generous man who had contributed large sums of money to the Separatist Church in Holland. He was traveling with his wife, Katherine, and five servants. One of the servants, John Howland, had been swept overboard during the journey and had survived by grabbing onto the rope used to raise and lower the upper sail, which was trailing in the water. He clung onto the rope, even as he was pulled 10 feet (3 m) below the water, until several strong sailors grabbed it and pulled him back onto the ship.

The ship's master sped as quickly as possible to Cape Cod Harbor (present-day Provincetown Harbor) on the tip of Cape Cod. By early morning on November 11, 1620, the *Mayflower* was safely

MAYFLOWER COMPACT

On November 11, 1620, the male colonists on board the *Mayflower* signed an agreement designed to bring an end to any talk of rebellion among the settlers and ensure that all would respect the basic laws needed to govern the colony. This document has come to be known as the Mayflower Compact:

IN THE NAME OF GOD, AMEN. We, whose names are underwritten, the Loyal Subjects of our dread Sovereign Lord King *James*, by the Grace of God, of *Great Britain*, *France*, and *Ireland*, King, *Defender of the Faith*, &c. Having undertaken for the Glory of God, and Advancement of the Christian Faith, and the Honour of our King and Country, a Voyage to plant the first Colony in the northern Parts of *Virginia*; Do by these Presents, solemnly and mutually, in the Presence of God and one another, covenant and combine ourselves together into a civil Body Politick, for our better Ordering and Preservation, and Furtherance of the Ends aforesaid: And by Virtue hereof do enact, constitute, and frame, such just and equal Laws, Ordinances, Acts, Constitutions, and Officers, from time to time, as shall be thought most meet and convenient for the general Good of the Colony; unto which we promise all due Submission and Obedience. IN WITNESS whereof we have hereunto subscribed our names at *Cape-Cod* the eleventh of November, in the Reign of our Sovereign Lord King *James*, of *England*, *France*, and *Ireland*, the eighteenth, and of *Scotland* the fifty-fourth. A.D. 1620.

anchored. Then, before anyone left the ship, all able-bodied men were required to sign the Compact. Those who could sign their name did so, beginning with the newly elected governor John Carver. Those who could not write their names put an "X" or some other mark on the document.

William Bradford and his fellow colonists had safely arrived in America. But they were hundreds of miles from the place they had intended to settle. They were 3,000 miles (4,828 km) from home, and more than 500 miles (804.7 km) from the closest English settlements. As Bradford noted in *Of Plymouth Plantation*, "Having thus passed the vast ocean, and that sea of troubles before while they were making their preparations, they now had no friends to welcome them, nor inns to entertain and refresh their weather beaten bodies, nor houses—much less towns—to repair to."

They did not know that within a year, 14 of the 19 women on board would die, including Bradford's wife. Six of the children, three of the young adults, and more than half the men also would not survive the first year. For now, they looked across the water, at what Bradford described as "a desolate wilderness," and made their preparations to go ashore.

2

A Young Man from Yorkshire

Thanks to the detailed journals he kept William Bradford ensured that the experiences of the Pilgrims were well documented. The rich narrative he recorded gives a vivid picture of his experience on the *Mayflower* as well as the colonists' efforts to build a new home in Plymouth.

But the early years of William Bradford's life before he set sail on the *Mayflower* were not as carefully recorded. The details of his childhood and youth are rather sketchy. He was born in March 1590; his family's church records his baptism as taking place on March 19, 1590.

Bradford was born in the small village of Austerfield, in the region of northern England known as Yorkshire. His family, like most people in the village, earned

William Bradford was baptized at the font of St. Helena Church in England (above) on March 19, 1590. Bradford's faith led him to challenge the teachings of the Church of England.

their living as farmers. His childhood was marked by tragedy. By the time he was 12 years old, both his parents and his sister had died as well as the grandfather who had cared for him after the death of his parents. He went to live with his two uncles, who expected him to help with farming chores. But shortly after the move he became so sick that he was no longer able to help in the fields. Bradford spent a long period recuperating and reading.

There were few books in the house. One book the family did have was a Bible. The so-called Geneva Bible, which was published less than 100 years before Bradford read it, was the first translation of the Bible into English. The experience of studying the Bible and poring over the notes and appendices to gain further insight would shape Bradford's understanding of his faith and challenge the teachings of the Church of England in which he had been raised.

THE SEPARATIST MOVEMENT

William Bradford's exploration of his faith came at a time when many in England were asking similar questions about the best way for a Christian to worship and to seek God's will. Many felt that the old practices of the Church of England (or Anglican Church), enforced by a hierarchy of bishops and priests, were corrupt and prevented proper worship. Nathaniel Philbrick describes in *Mayflower*, "a typical Sunday service in England—in which parishioners stared dumbly at a minister mumbling incomprehensible phrases from the Book of Common Prayer." This Book of Common Prayer was another subject of contention. It was first introduced in the mid-1500s and contained Biblical text and paraphrases of Biblical text, with words and prayers repeated week after week during worship services.

For supporters of the Church of England, the centuries of tradition and the education and training of Anglican priests provided an important addition to what was found in the Bible. They felt it helped worshippers to better understand the teachings of their faith. But a growing number of people in England believed that these traditions interfered with the Bible's original meaning. Their objections were not simply a form of religious protest, however. The head of the Church of England was the English monarch. During Bradford's youth that was Queen Elizabeth I until 1603, and after Elizabeth's death it was King James I. There was little tolerance for the protests from a group that came to be known as Puritans for their efforts to purify the church and its leadership.

For the Puritans, the key to worship lay in the Bible. Anything not directly taken from the Bible was man-made. Hymns were a

KING JAMES I

The actions of King James I launched a series of events that ultimately led to the founding of the colony at Plymouth. Under King James, religious persecution of the Separatists greatly increased in England, inspiring William Bradford and the other members of his congregation to flee to Holland. It was King James who first issued a charter to settle the territory in America known as Virginia, including the colony at Jamestown that would bear his name. It was to King James that Bradford and his fellow Separatists would petition to obtain the right to settle in America, and found the colony that would become Plymouth.

James was born in 1566, the son of Mary Queen of Scots and her second husband, Henry Stewart. His father was murdered by opponents of his mother when he was only a few months old. Queen Mary was forced to abdicate the Scottish throne when James was only 13 months old and fled to England. She was imprisoned there for nearly 20 years before she was executed. James's childhood was marked by palace intrigue, violence, civil war, and a succession of regents who ruled in his place until he was 18 years old. He then married Anne of Denmark, with whom he had nine children.

corruption because words and phrases from the scripture were often changed to fit a rhyme or melody. There was no mention of bishops in the Bible, so the Puritans lobbied for the system of bishops to be eliminated. Puritans disregarded the common practices in the Anglican Church of reading from the Book of Common Prayer, making the sign of the cross, and kneeling during communion. They believed in the idea of predestiny; that God had already selected his "chosen people" who would be saved. These people would be obvious to all

A treaty signed with his cousin, Queen Elizabeth I of England, meant that he inherited the English throne when the childless and unmarried queen died in 1603. He then moved to England and ruled both England and Scotland from there, claiming for himself the title James I, King of Great Britain.

Tensions between England and Scotland and James's outspoken belief in the rights of kings (as well as his extravagant spending) marked his reign with unrest and challenges. Religious protests added to the difficulties, not only from Puritans but also from Catholics.

But James's role in firmly supporting the Church of England against external challenges ultimately inspired the Puritan and Separatist exodus, first to Holland and later to America. He commissioned an English version of the Bible, the so-called King James version, which would be the standard English-language Bible for more than 250 years. And his support of efforts to colonize America led to the expansion of the British Empire and the founding of the colony of Virginia.

James I died on March 27, 1625, less than five years after the *Mayflower* reached Plymouth.

because of the godly life they lived. You could not be sure whether or not you were among the saved—or "Saints" as the Puritans called them—but if you lived a good and holy life, your behavior showed signs that you were one of these "Saints."

The Puritans can be loosely divided into two groups: those who wanted to purify the Church of England from within while remaining part of it, and those who wanted to separate from the church and start again. William Bradford joined the latter group in his mid-teens.

How Bradford learned of the small group of Separatists meeting in the tiny town of Scrooby, several miles from his home, is not clear. He must have demonstrated trustworthiness to some member of the group, however, since what this group was doing was illegal.

With the ascent of King James I to the English throne, the persecution of Separatist groups increased. In *The Times of their Lives: Life, Love, and Death in Plymouth Colony*, authors James Deetz and Patricia Scott Deetz quote the king's famous complaint against the Separatists: "I will make them conform, or I will harry them out of the land!" Several well-known Separatist ministers were executed, and the secrecy around Separatist gatherings became even more critical.

The Separatist group in Scrooby that Bradford joined was formed in 1606, when he was about 16 years old. The congregation met at the home of the Scrooby postmaster, William Brewster, where they were led in worship every Sunday by one of two ministers. The minister would give a sermon, and then members of the congregation would share their thoughts on important spiritual teachings or religious doctrine; a service would generally last several hours.

In the tight-knit community, deeply committed to their religious beliefs, Bradford found a strong connection and a substitute family. But it was a family that was engaged in an illegal activity, and by 1607 the existence of the Scrooby congregation came to the attention of the authorities. Several members of the congregation were put in prison and others were placed under surveillance.

The congregation decided to leave England for Holland, where they could worship freely. But this, too, had to be done secretly. At the time, anyone traveling from England to Europe needed official permission in the form of a license, and these licenses were not granted to those leaving the country for religious reasons. But 17-year-old William Bradford was determined to follow the group's leaders,

Bradford found a family in the Scrooby Separatists, but his connection with the group resulted in imprisonment. It became clear they could not worship as they pleased in England. *Above*, a cell in the prison where the Separatists were held on their first attempt to sail to Holland.

including William Brewster and the minister John Robinson, to a new home.

FLIGHT TO HOLLAND

The Scrooby congregation hired a ship's captain to smuggle them across the English Channel to Holland. But once they and their possessions were on board the ship, the captain betrayed them to the authorities. Their possessions were seized, the money they had brought with them to start their new life was taken, and they were thrown into prison. After a month Bradford and a few of the others were released, but seven of the congregation's leaders remained in prison for several months.

In the spring of 1608 they again attempted to flee to Holland. This time they hired a Dutch captain, who agreed to smuggle them to his country. The plan called for the group to travel to the Humber River, near the town of Grimsby on England's eastern coast. They would meet the captain there, load themselves and their possessions onto his boat, and sail to Holland.

But once again the Separatists' plans were thwarted. They successfully met the captain and several of the men had climbed on board when a local militia appeared. The Dutch captain, fearing arrest, quickly set course for Amsterdam and sailed away. No women or children made it on board, nor had the possessions been loaded. Many families were separated. Husbands who had boarded watched as their wives and children were left behind to be captured by the authorities. It was a fearful time for those on board. They had little money and no possessions. And those left behind had no homes to return to, having sold their property in anticipation of starting a new life abroad. It would be several months before everyone would be reunited in Holland.

From Bradford's journal, it is clear that he was one of those on board the ship when it sailed away. He describes a terrible storm at sea, and a crossing that took 14 days, "in seven of which they saw neither sun, moon, nor stars, being driven near the coast of Norway." Bradford records a frightening moment when the sailors began to panic, crying out, "We sink, we sink!" as water rushed over the side of the boat.

They eventually arrived in Holland, and by 1609 a total of 125 members of the Scrooby congregation were in Amsterdam, including Bradford and William Brewster, and the two ministers, Richard Clyfton and John Robinson. Several other Separatist groups had similarly sought refuge in Amsterdam, and soon these different groups were quarreling over proper practices and teachings.

On February 12, 1609, the congregation filed a formal application with the government in Holland to establish their home in the city of Leiden, to the south of Amsterdam, in part to avoid becoming caught up in these disputes. After a year in Amsterdam, the majority of the congregation moved, many of them choosing to live in a small enclave of homes behind John Robinson's house.

Bradford describes Leiden (or "Leyden," as he calls it in *Of Plymouth Plantation*) as "a fair and beautiful city, of a sweet situation, made famous by its university." At the time of Bradford's arrival there, Leiden was a commercial city of some 40,000 people. The Scrooby congregation had lived in a small village in England where most of them earned a living by farming. In the bustling city of Leiden they were forced to find work in factories or doing some other form of menial labor. The pace of life was far more hectic; a typical workweek lasted six days, from dawn to dusk, with men, women, and children all expected to work.

While in Leiden, Bradford began to emerge as a leader of the church. At the age of 21 he inherited family property in England, which he sold. The money paid for a small house in Leiden. Bradford had found work as a *fustian*, or corduroy worker—"fustian" was a kind of strong cotton fabric—and in 1612 he officially became a citizen of Leiden. One year later, he married Dorothy May, and in 1617 they had a son, John.

PLANS FOR A JOURNEY

Bradford and the others had lived in Holland for about 12 years when they began to discuss the possibility of leaving. Their life in Holland had been marked by hard labor, and because they lived such a separate life, by choice, it was difficult for them to feel truly at home in their new country. Their numbers were not growing; in fact, few people chose to join them and they saw little chance of improving their finances or gaining better employment if they remained in Holland. There were rumors of war between Holland and Spain, which led to concerns that if war should break out there would be greater restrictions on foreigners living in Holland. This could affect the work that was available and their ability to worship freely.

Of perhaps greater concern to many of the original Scrooby congregation was that their children, after 12 years in Holland, viewed themselves as Dutch rather than English. There were more temptations in the bustling city of Leiden, and many of the children chose to abandon the strict religious practices of their parents.

Bradford's group decided that the time had come to move again. This time they would go where they could build their own colony, shaping a homeland where they could own their own land, prosper economically, and worship freely. "The place they fixed their thoughts upon was somewhere in those vast and unpeopled countries of America," Bradford wrote.

They debated where in America to settle. Bradford notes that the discussions included Guyana (a British colony in South America), the Caribbean Islands, and "Virginia" (the broad term for the eastern coast of America south of New England). The argument in favor of Guyana and a tropical colony was that the land was rich and fruitful, the weather was always warm, and there would be abundant food. But some argued that a tropical climate would mean unfamiliar diseases and pests, as well as threats from nearby Spanish colonies.

There had been some early—though largely unsuccessful—English settlements in the territory known as "Virginia," and this was both a plus and a minus for the Separatists. The greatest fear was that, should they establish a colony among or close to the other English settlements, they would once again face the same kind of religious persecution they had known in England.

Finally it was decided that they should try to establish their own, separate colony within the Virginia territory but far away from the established settlements. Next, they needed to obtain King James's approval for their efforts, and financial backing for the voyage.

The financial backing was a key part of the planning. France, Holland, and Spain had funded expeditions to the New World, but in England the financial backing for colonies was provided not by the government, but instead by private companies. In 1606 King James had chartered the Virginia Company, whose mission was to finance the settlement of Virginia by appointing governing officials, and providing settlers, ships, and supplies. The company's initial attempts to found colonies, particularly in Jamestown, had been disappointing financially, and gradually the company changed to a policy of issuing patents to those interested in establishing a colony. Settlers would be given a conditional patent that gave them the right to attempt to found a colony. They had five to seven years to make a success of it; they could then apply for a new patent that would give them the permanent right to settle the land.

Two members of the congregation—John Carver and Robert Cushman—were sent to London to negotiate with the Virginia

Company and obtain the patent. The company granted the patent in June of 1619. William Bradford was so committed to the enterprise that he sold his house in Leiden that spring in anticipation of making the voyage. But while the congregation now had a patent that gave them the right to attempt to found a colony, they did not yet have the financial resources to make the journey possible.

As the Separatists looked for a financial backer for their trip, they learned of a congregation much like their own, a group of 180 English Separatists who had sailed from Holland to found their own colony. By the time they reached America, 130 of them were dead, victims of disease and dehydration from lack of freshwater. This grim news caused many of the Leiden congregation to rethink their plans.

Bradford's group finally found financial backing. A group of London investors known as the Merchant Adventurers granted them a loan. These 70 wealthy businessmen were interested in financing the establishment of colonies in America both as an investment opportunity and for religious reasons. Thomas Weston, who represented the Merchant Adventurers proposed a joint venture. The majority of the financing provided by the Adventurers would be repaid out of the profits the Separatists would make through cod fishing and fur trading. As part of the agreement, the settlers would work four days a week for the company, two days a week for themselves, and would have one day—the Sabbath—reserved for rest and worship. At the end of the seven years the profits of the venture would be divided among everyone, and the settlers would own their homes and land. The settlement would be in the northern section of "Virginia," far from other English settlements, located at the mouth of the Hudson River.

CHOOSING THE FIRST WAVE

The members of the congregation discussed who would travel to America and who would remain behind. It was decided that everyone

After 12 years in Holland, it became clear that the Separatists needed to find another place to live. Finally, in July 1620, the pilgrims said an emotional goodbye to their friends and families and boarded the *Mayflower*.

would not go at the same time. The strongest and most enthusiastic would go first, as they would have the hardest task of clearing the land and building the settlement. It was clear that some were more fit for the demands and the rigors of building a colony than others and some needed to sell their homes and make preparations before they could leave.

Bradford was in the first group, having sold his home nearly a year earlier in anticipation of the voyage. About a third of the congregation (125 people) was in this first group of settlers. The minister, John Robinson, would stay behind with the larger group, while

William Brewster would provide spiritual guidance to the group traveling to America.

A departure date was set for the spring of 1620, and as the plans grew firmer their financial backer, Thomas Weston, began to change the terms of their agreement. He had been unable to obtain a fishing monopoly for the settlement, and without the promise of high profit from fishing, some of the Merchant Adventurers, Weston claimed, were reluctant to fund the settlement. The only solution was for the colonists to agree to work full time for the company; they would no longer have two days a week to work for themselves. There also was no longer a clause that granted each settler the right to his own home and land at the end of the seven years; instead all property would now be owned jointly by the settlers. This caused "much trouble and contention," as Bradford noted, particularly when the congregation in Leiden learned that Robert Cushman had already agreed to Weston's demands. They were disturbed at the news that the Adventurers intended to include non-Separatists from London with their group. They debated about how these "Strangers" would mix with them and whether or not they would respect their religious beliefs.

As spring gave way to summer, the colonists grew even angrier when they learned that Thomas Weston had not yet arranged for transportation to America. They had planned to arrive in America when the weather was still warm and they could plant crops for the following year and build shelters before winter set in. Many had already sold their homes. They needed to leave as soon as possible.

While responsibility for hiring a ship large enough to transport most of the settlers remained with Weston, the Leiden congregation bought a small ship in Holland, giving it the name *Speedwell*. This small ship could carry some of the settlers across the Atlantic, but more critically it could be used for fishing and exploration once they had settled in their new home. It would also provide them with a means to leave America if something disastrous should happen. They hired a master and crew, who agreed to stay in America for at least a year.

Supplies were purchased by Cushman and Carver for the journey, including salted beef and pork, beer, wine, and dried peas. They bought fishing supplies, tools, muskets, and armor, as well as goods to be used for trading with the Indians.

Finally, in late July, the first group of settlers, accompanied by family and friends, traveled to the Dutch port of Delfshaven, where they were to board the *Speedwell* and sail to Southampton in England. There they would meet up with Weston and many would transfer to the larger ship Weston had hired, a vessel called the *Mayflower*.

"Truly doleful was the sight of that sad and mournful parting," Bradford wrote. "What sighs and sobs and prayers rose from amongst them!" For William and Dorothy Bradford it must have been a sad parting, indeed, for they had decided to leave their three-year-old son, John, behind in Holland. They probably felt that he would be safer in Amsterdam with Dorothy's parents than facing the unknown dangers of America.

It was William Bradford who first used the phrase that would come to define these settlers as they left friends and family behind and prepared to sail to a new world. "They knew they were pilgrims," he wrote, "and lifted up their eyes to the heavens, their dearest country, and quieted their spirits."

3

The New Land

The "desolate wilderness" that William Bradford described may have been unfamiliar territory to Bradford and the other settlers, but it was neither unknown to Europeans nor uninhabited. The Italian explorer Giovanni da Verrazano had sailed into Narragansett Bay, near modern Rhode Island, in 1524, nearly a hundred years before the *Mayflower* sailed along Cape Cod. English explorer Bartholomew Gosnold had named the cape in the early 1600s for the schools of cod that swam through its waters, prompting regular voyages by European cod-fishing ships to harvest the fish during the summers. Gosnold built a small fort at the southwestern corner of the cape. Gosnold and da Verrazano encountered Native Americans, whom they referred to as Indians. In Gosnold's case the Indians arrived first to trade, but gradually grew hostile, forcing him to abandon his fort and his plans for a trading post.

In 1605 Samuel de Champlain of France began exploring the cape and creating detailed maps of some of its harbors and inlets. In 1611 the English explorer Edward Harlow arrived. He was prepared for a hostile welcome from the Indians; he and his crew fought brutally against the native population, killing many and kidnapping five, one of whom he then took back with him to England to put on public display.

An English attempt to build a settlement on the coast of Maine failed after less than a year. The colonists abandoned their efforts after hostility from Indians and a harsh winter. The region had gained a reputation for inhospitable weather and natives, but Captain John Smith decided to mount an expedition there in 1614.

Smith was a veteran of the efforts to establish colonies in America, having been involved in the colony at Jamestown in Virginia. For a portion of 1608 and 1609 Smith had been in charge of Jamestown. Previously the Jamestown settlers had focused on searching for gold and other precious metals in the region, rather than engaging in the planting of crops and building shelters that was necessary for their survival. As a result, many of the original colonists died. Under Smith's command, that all changed. The colonists were forced to spend six hours a day working in the fields. For the first time the previously chaotic colony was brought under control and the starvation that had plagued it was held at bay.

But Smith's strict control sparked bitter complaints among the men at Jamestown, and he was eventually forced out of the colony. A period of starvation followed his departure. The adventurers who sailed for the New World expecting to find streets paved with gold and easy wealth once again failed to plant the crops needed for their survival.

Smith later mounted an expedition to explore territories north of Jamestown, with several ships forming part of his fleet. It was John Smith who named the region "New England," claiming, according

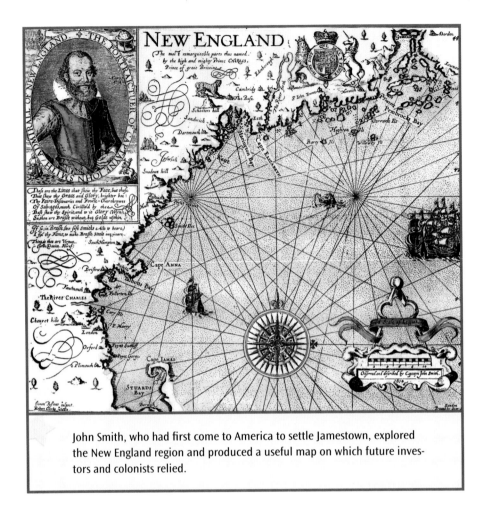

John Smith, who had first come to America to settle Jamestown, explored the New England region and produced a useful map on which future investors and colonists relied.

to Alan Taylor in *American Colonies*, that its climate and soil closely resembled that of England. Smith explored the region and returned to his homeland with promotional material and a map. The Pilgrims purchased these materials before their voyage. In fact, Smith had offered to return with the Pilgrims, to serve as a guide and help them establish a colony in New England. But the Pilgrims refused his offer, believing that his strong ideas and personality would interfere with their ability to establish the colony they wanted—a colony based on religious principles.

While exploring the region, the commander of one of Smith's ships, Thomas Hunt, decided to capture as many of the native population as he could. He took 24 men back across the Atlantic and sold them as slaves in Spain. When a French ship landed on the north shore of Cape Cod a year later, the Indians responded in kind, capturing the French sailors (whose ship had been damaged) and killing all but a few. The survivors were kept as slaves.

One year before the *Mayflower* sailed to America, an English explorer named Thomas Dermer reached the coast of Maine and then began to head south. With him was a guide named Squanto who knew the region well. Squanto was one of the Indians who had been seized and kidnapped by Thomas Hunt five years earlier. Having spent time in Spain and England, Squanto was at last returning home to the site of what would become the Plymouth colony.

Squanto was anticipating his return to a thriving Indian settlement of some 2,000 people. This group had farmed the region, gathered fish from its shores, and settled in mobile communities that traveled with the seasons. They planted fields in the spring, spent time along the coast in the summer to fish, harvested crops in the fall, and then moved inland when the winter grew harsh. But what Squanto found as he led Dermer south was a series of empty villages. The population had been devastated by illness brought by the Europeans who had come to the region to explore and trade. Most Europeans were somewhat resistant to these diseases, which included plague and smallpox. But these diseases were unknown in America and the native populations were swiftly devastated by them. Dermer and his crew eventually fell under attack; Squanto was taken prisoner and only Dermer (who had been wounded) and one other Englishman managed to escape. They attempted to flee south to Virginia, but Dermer died from his wounds before they reached their destination.

The history of the contact between Europeans and Native Americans leading up to the arrival of the Pilgrims was marked by disease, conflict, and misunderstanding. According to Nathan Philbrick's *Mayflower*, when the Pilgrims first arrived the Native Americans assumed they had come to avenge the attack on Dermer.

FIRST TRIP ASHORE

The *Mayflower* had anchored at the northernmost tip of Cape Cod, in the harbor of what would become Provincetown. It was Saturday, November 11, 1620. After the passengers signed the Mayflower Compact, a group of 16 armed men were chosen from among the passengers to explore the land.

Accounts differ as to exactly when this exploration took place. In *The Times of Their Lives*, the authors suggest that the group first went ashore on November 11, right after signing the Compact. They gathered wood, took a look around, and returned to the ship without meeting any native inhabitants. But William Bradford's journal states that the first exploration took place on November 15 because the small boat that was to transport the group from the *Mayflower* to shore had been damaged on the journey and needed repair.

Anticipating danger, the men were equipped with armor and weapons, a musket and sword. They were rowed as close to shore as possible, but the shallowness along the coast meant that they had to then wade through the icy November water to reach the beach. Bradford, who was one of the 16 men in that initial group, wrote that they had marched along the shore for about a mile when they saw "five or six persons with a dog coming towards them." Realizing that these were Indians, the Pilgrims quickly ran after them. Hampered by their heavy armor, the Pilgrims were soon outdistanced, but they followed the Indians' tracks through the sand for several miles.

When it grew dark, they stopped and set up a rotation of three guards at a time. The others tried to sleep, resting around a large fire.

Captain Miles Standish was in charge. He was responsible for handling military matters as the Pilgrims set up their colony.

The next morning, Standish ordered the men to continue tracking the Indians. They followed the trail to a point where the Indians left the beach and turned into the woods. There the tracks disappeared, and the Pilgrims attempted to guess where they had gone, gradually wandering into woods so thick that their clothes and armor were damaged.

The long march had left them tired and thirsty. Finally they stumbled across a freshwater spring where, according to Bradford, they "refreshed themselves with the first New England water they had drunk; and in their great thirst they found it as pleasant as wine or beer had been before."

After a long drink, they found their way back to the shoreline. The *Mayflower* was visible in the distance, northwest of where they stood. They built a large fire—a signal to those on board to show where the explorers were and that they were still alive—and settled in for the night, taking turns to serve as guards and to rest.

Their exploration continued the next day, where in a large patch of cleared land they could see areas where the Indians had once planted corn. They also found evidence of Indian graves—small mounds marked by a bow and several rotted arrows.

As they continued to march south, they discovered an area where the sand appeared to have been disturbed and then patted smooth. Three men began to dig, while the others kept guard in case they had been lured into a trap. In the sand pit they found a reed basket filled with a large amount of dried Indian corn. There was also a basket with ears of corn in various colors, perfectly preserved in its dried state.

On board the *Mayflower* the Pilgrims had wheat, barley, and peas to plant in the spring. But the corn seed seemed providential to these settlers whose provisions were meager. After a brief discussion, they

MILES STANDISH

Miles (also Myles) Standish was born in 1584 in England, either in Lancashire or the Isle of Man; the precise location is not known. He was a short man, nicknamed Captain Shrimp, according to Francis Dillon's *The Pilgrims*, with red hair and a ruddy complexion. He served in the English army and eventually was sent to Holland as part of a small fighting force that Queen Elizabeth I had ordered to help the Dutch in a skirmish with Spain. While in Holland he met the Pilgrim's minister, John Robinson. Standish was not a member of Robinson's congregation but he must have maintained his ties to Robinson and the Pilgrims. As plans for their new settlement in America were made, Captain Standish was quickly hired to serve as the new colony's military leader. He was to help coordinate the group's defense against Native American threats as well as any threats from foreign powers, specifically the French, Spanish, or Dutch.

Standish sailed on board the *Mayflower* with his wife, Rose. Sadly, she died during the Pilgrims' first few months at Plymouth. Standish was one of the few who did not become sick during those early, dangerous months. In fact, he helped care for many of those who were ailing. He led the efforts to explore the area along Cape Cod, helping to select the eventual choice for the settlement site.

Standish was known for his quick temper, but despite conflicts with several of the colonists he became one of the most influential members of Plymouth Colony. He was involved in ongoing negotiations with the Merchant Adventurers, who had financed the colony, and made several trading trips to England once the colony was established. He led several trading and military expeditions to Indian camps as well as an attack on Indians living in the Massachusetts Bay area who were thought to be plotting against the Plymouth colonists. His violent response in that attack—killing and executing several Indians—brought strong criticism from many in the colony.

His second wife, Barbara, was part of a subsequent wave of settlers that arrived at Plymouth in 1623 on board the ship *Anne*. They married a few months after she landed at Plymouth and ultimately had seven children.

In the mid-1630s Standish led a group of settlers who helped found the town of Duxbury. He and his family remained there and Standish died in Duxbury in 1656.

Standish was immortalized in a poem by Henry Wadsworth Longfellow, "The Courtship of Miles Standish," written in 1858. The poem tells of a love triangle between Standish, John Alden, and Priscilla Mullins. In Longfellow's version, shortly after the death of Standish's first wife, Rose, Standish fell in love with Priscilla Mullins. At the time, he was sharing a home with John Alden, and he sent Alden to speak with Priscilla to see if she would consent to marry Standish. Alden speaks so eloquently and romantically that, in Longfellow's poem, Priscilla instead replies, "Why don't you speak for yourself, John?" Standish is left tragically disappointed in love when his roommate wins Priscilla's hand.

Longfellow certainly dramatized events to better suit his poetry, but historical records do show that both Priscilla Mullins and John Alden lived at Plymouth and were married sometime before 1623. Alden helped found the town of Duxbury, along with Standish, and years later John and Priscilla Alden's daughter, Sarah, married Alexander Standish, the son of Miles and Barbara.

decided to take the corn. They poured as much as they could into a kettle. The result was so heavy that two men were needed to carry it back to the ship. Bradford notes that they intended to repay the Indians for the corn whenever they could meet with them, and he described it as "a great mercy to this poor people, that they thus got seed to plant corn the next year, or they might have starved; for they had none, nor any likelihood of getting any, till too late for the planting season."

They spent one more night along the shore, this time in the cold November rain. They made a makeshift shelter from branches, and the next morning continued their exploration, this time to the north. Once more they became lost in the woods. In the trees they spotted an Indian deer trap—a rope surrounding some acorns attached to a young tree that was bent to the ground. William Bradford was in the rear of the group; as he moved forward he stumbled and fell into the trap. The tree instantly sprang up and Bradford was jerked up by the leg. Bradford was not annoyed; instead he admired the craftsmanship of the trap. He was set free, and the group took the trap with them as they headed back to the harbor. There a small boat awaited them and they were rowed back to the *Mayflower*.

ICY EXPLORATION

On December 6 they set out again in the small boat. This time five members of the *Mayflower*'s crew went with 10 of the Pilgrims. Freezing temperatures and illness were beginning to affect many. The ship's master, Christopher Jones, was anxious for the Pilgrims to decide where to locate their settlement so that shelter could be prepared for those who were sick and his ship could return to England.

Bradford was once more one of the explorers. He wrote of weather so cold that as they set out in the small boat, "the spray of the sea froze on their coats like glass." They rowed into an area known as Wellfleet Bay. On the shore they saw about 12 Indians busy with something, but they had some difficulty with the shallow waters and by the time they had waded ashore it was nearly dark and the Indians had disappeared. They built a barricade of log and tree branches and once more took turns serving as guards or sleeping around the large fire. At some point in the night they could see the smoke of an Indian fire, about four miles away.

The next morning they set out to explore. Their focus was on finding the best location for their new home. Winter was beginning and they needed to start building shelters as quickly as possible.

They came to the place where they had seen the Indians working the previous day and found the remains of a whale, from which the Indians had apparently been cutting strips of blubber. Whales routinely became stranded along this part of the cape; they found two more dead whales as they continued their exploration. They spent all day moving along the shore, some in the small boat that had transported them from the *Mayflower* and others on land, but they found no place suitable. The two groups met up at night near a creek, known today as Herring River, where once more they built a barricade from logs and thick pine branches, as tall as a man, to provide shelter from the icy wind and some protection if they should come under attack. Then they built a fire in the middle and those who were not on guard duty lay down around the fire to sleep.

Some time around midnight they were awakened by a "hideous cry," in Bradford's words, and the shouts of the guards calling out, "Arm, arm!" They grabbed their weapons, and some of the men fired the muskets. It was then quiet. One of the sailors reassured the other men that he had heard similar noises from wolves when he was exploring Newfoundland. They drifted back to sleep until about five o' clock the next morning.

After a time of prayer, they prepared for another day of exploring. Some of the men carried their weapons and armor down to the water, placing them next to the boat and then returning to the camp for breakfast. As they were eating, they again heard the hideous cry—the same horrifying noise they had heard the previous night.

One of the men ran into the barricade where the others were breakfasting, crying out, "Men; Indians, Indians!" at which point several arrows flew into the barricade. The four men who still had their weapons quickly grabbed them; those who had unluckily carried them down to the boat raced across the sand toward their weapons. They were swiftly trapped behind the boat and forced to take shelter there.

In *Mayflower*, Nathaniel Philbrick notes that the weapons most of the men carried were matchlocks—muskets equipped with long burning wicks that were used to ignite the gun's priming powder. The powder had to be kept dry in order to fire properly; this became a challenge in the chilly, wet spray that blew off the water. In order to fire the gun, the men had to first dip the wick into the campfire and then, once it was lit, they could begin firing. But the process was slow and cumbersome, far slower than the Indians fired arrows.

Once armed, the men began blasting away with their matchlocks while the Indians rained a continuous stream of arrows upon them. One large Indian stood behind a tree a short distance from the barricade, sending arrow after arrow flying into it. The Pilgrims fired three times at him without success, until finally they managed to hit the tree he was hiding behind. As bark splintered around him, he cried out and ran into the woods with the other Indians following him. The Pilgrims left a small group of armed men to guard the boat and attempted to follow the Indians without success. Finally, they shot off two or three muskets as a sign of defiance and returned to their camp. They gathered several of the arrows that had been fired at them and later sent them back to England when the *Mayflower* made its return journey. Bradford notes that they named that place "The First Encounter," a name the beach (in present-day Eastham) still carries today.

The Indians of the Plymouth area had already been exposed to European explorers and settlers by the time the passengers of the *Mayflower* arrived at their shores. The first encounter between the local Native Americans and the Plymouth colonists served to frighten both parties.

A SAFE HARBOR

The Pilgrims decided to return to their boat and continue their search for a settlement site from the deck. They sailed along Cape Cod Bay's southern edge for several hours, seeking a harbor that one of the sailors promised them he remembered seeing nearby. It began to rain and then to snow; in the middle of the afternoon the wind picked up, and the water became very choppy. The rudder broke and two men were forced to stand in the stern of the boat holding long oars and trying to steer the boat in the proper direction. After dark, the freezing rain and snow chilled all of them. The mast splintered into three pieces and the sail tumbled into the choppy water.

The frozen men pulled the heavy sail out of the icy water, then grabbed for oars and did their best to row to shore, risking capsizing as they neared a rock-strewn beach that the sailor—who had earlier promised them safe passage to a familiar harbor—now declared he had never seen before. They rowed as hard as they could around the rocks and managed to maneuver their boat around the tip of what they later discovered was an island.

On the far side of the island the water calmed, although an icy rain was still falling. The men debated what to do next. Some, fearing another Indian attack, wanted to stay in the boat. But others were tired, wet, and cold and finally they all decided to risk an encounter in order to dry themselves by a fire.

Fortunately, there was no further attack. In the morning—"a fair sun-shining day," in Bradford's words—they discovered that they were on an uninhabited, wooded island. Because John Clark, one of the *Mayflower*'s pilots, was the first to set foot there, it became known as Clark's Island. They decided to spend the day there, drying their equipment and armor, and cutting down a tree to repair the mast. The following day, a Sunday, they rested and worshipped, and then continued their explorations of the region on Monday.

They found that their island was on the western edge of a harbor, well sheltered and yet large enough to accommodate a ship the size of the *Mayflower*. They were northwest of Cape Cod; they sailed across the harbor to determine its depth and the ease of maneuvering, then landed on the shore of what would become Plymouth. They found running brooks and cornfields—evidence that the land had been cultivated by Indians at some point—but no signs of recent occupation. It was, Bradford wrote, "a place, as they supposed, fit for a settlement, at least it was the best they could find, and considering the season of the year and their present necessity they were thankful for it."

On Tuesday, December 12, they returned to the *Mayflower* with the welcome news that a site for their new settlement had been found. But the returning explorers quickly learned that tragedy had struck while they were finding a new home. Five days earlier, 23-year-old Dorothy Bradford—William Bradford's wife—had fallen over the side of the *Mayflower* and drowned.

4

The Plymouth Settlement

William Bradford makes no mention of the tragic death of Dorothy, his wife of seven years, in *Of Plymouth Plantation*. Instead, his account of that time only notes the gladness of those on board the ship upon learning that a site for their settlement had been found.

On December 15 the *Mayflower* weighed anchor and attempted to sail to Plymouth Harbor, but strong winds prevented them from entering the harbor. Instead, the ship anchored about a mile and a half away, near the end of what is known as Long Beach. Now that the Pilgrims were all together, they spent three days exploring the area around the harbor and debating the precise location of their settlement. Some voted for a return to Clark's Island, believing that it would be the safest spot to defend against hostile Indians. Others favored a location on a river directly across the harbor from the island, which they named Jones River after the ship's master. However, the river was not deep enough for a ship even half the size of the *Mayflower* to sail up, and it offered little protection should Indians choose to attack.

Finally, on Wednesday, December 20, 1620, the Pilgrims decided where their new home would be. They selected a site near the shore where a 165-foot (50.3-m) hill offered clear views of the surrounding area along the coast as far as Cape Cod, some 30 miles (48.3 km) away. A fort on the top of this hill could provide strong security against any attacks by sea or land. There was a brook nearby large enough to accommodate small boats, and a wide salt marsh where boats could be left in harbor. There were freshwater springs near the brook. The land had already been cleared by Indians, but there was no evidence that any were still living in the region. The Pilgrims did not know that this was due to the illness and disease that had devastated the native population several years earlier.

They chose a site on the flat ground on the north side of the brook. The hill would provide an ideal spot for the cannons they had brought with them.

On December 25, 1620, they began building the first house at Plymouth. It was Christmas Day, but the Pilgrims viewed the traditional Christmas celebrations as pagan feasts, and instead a full working crew of Pilgrims busied themselves cutting down trees with saws and axes to erect the frame of their first building—a 20-foot-square (6-m-square) "common house" for general use. Nathaniel Philbrick speculates that the house would have been similar to the cottages of rural England—walls made of tree trunks interwoven with branches and cemented together with clay. The roof would have been thatched, using reeds from the nearby marsh, while the few tiny windows would have been covered with a kind of linseed-coated parchment. The floor would have been dirt.

On December 28 the Pilgrims began working on their defense, following Captain Miles Standish's direction. They built a wooden platform at the top of the high hill for the cannons that had been brought on the *Mayflower*. They also began planning out the community they had named New Plimoth.

The plan that was sketched out involved two rows of houses and a cross street. They decided that all single men would find a family with whom to live at the beginning. The result was a decision to build 19 houses once they completed the common house. Each man had responsibility for building his own home rather than everyone working together to build each house. It was thought that the men would work faster to build their own homes than if they were working to build someone else's house first.

The street on which the houses would be built, known today as Leyden Street, was located on the north bank of the brook. It ran up to the foot of the hill on which the cannons were being mounted. Lots were marked off on each side of this street. In *The Pilgrims*, Francis Dillon explains that lots were marked off in narrow spaces, 8 by 49½ feet (2.4 by 15 m), and each person was entitled to a single lot. If a family had six members, they would receive six lots.

A kind of lottery was held for the sites. Only Miles Standish (who was given land space closest to the planned fort on top of the hill) and the governor, John Carver (who was given a larger corner plot), did not participate in the lottery. The Pilgrims then began to work as quickly as possible to build the houses.

SICKNESS AND SORROW

The Pilgrims had spent several months on board the *Mayflower* and now, as the new year began, they were spending a harsh January winter outdoors, cutting down trees and attempting to build homes. Their diet had not changed—they were still eating the dried and salted food they had brought with them on the ship. Scurvy soon began to spread among them as did pneumonia and tuberculosis.

On Thursday, January 11, 1621, William Bradford collapsed while working. He was taken to the common house, and some feared that he would not survive that first night. Quickly others became sick until the common house became a kind of infirmary. So many became ill that only six or seven people were left to care for those who were suffering—fetching wood to keep a fire burning, preparing meals, washing the clothes and sheets, and emptying chamber pots. Bradford specifically mentions William Brewster, who was to serve as the Pilgrims' spiritual leader, and Miles Standish as two who remained healthy throughout this epidemic and "spared no pains night nor day, but with abundance of toil and hazard of their own health" cared for Bradford and the others who were ill.

So many died during this time that far fewer houses were needed than they had originally planned. Instead of 19, only 7 houses were built that first year, once those who survived were sufficiently recovered to resume their construction. Bradford wrote, "in two or three months' time half of their company died, especially in January and February," sometimes as many as two or three a day. Four entire families died; only five of the eighteen wives survived. More than half of the servants and single men died. The Pilgrims did not want the Indians to know how many of them had fallen victim to illness, so the dead were taken out quietly at night and buried in unmarked graves.

During his illness, Bradford found himself craving a beer, and sent a message to the *Mayflower*, pleading that the sailors grant him this favor from their meager supplies. Word came back that even "if he were their own father he should have none." The sailors were now beginning to worry that they would not have enough supplies for their return voyage to England, and as the Pilgrims fell victim to illness and death, construction of the settlement stopped. The sailors stayed away from the settlement, but the infection soon spread on board, claiming many of the crew as victims. Bradford notes that the spread of the disease among the crew sparked a change of heart in the master, and Jones soon sent a message to the settlement that those who needed beer were now welcome to it, even if it meant that he and his crew would drink only water on their return journey.

On January 14 a spark from a fire spread to the thatched roof of the common house, where Bradford and the others were lying ill. As the only complete shelter, the common house was not only providing housing for those who were sick, but also for the settlement's supply of gunpowder, much of it in open barrels. As the flames spread overhead, Bradford and the others got up from their sick beds and moved the barrels of gunpowder outside, then attempted to beat out the flames. They succeeded in saving the basic timber structure of the building before collapsing back in their beds.

It was a desperate time, one made more uncertain by fears that Indians were nearby and might move in while most of the settlers were weak and sick. Master Jones reported seeing two Indians watching the ship from Clark's Island. At another point, one of the Pilgrims, who had gone out to hunt ducks, spotted 12 Indians moving toward the settlement. He quickly ran to find Miles Standish, who was working in the woods with another man, Francis Cook. Standish and Cook dropped their tools and ran down the hill to grab their weapons. The Indians never appeared at the settlement, but when Standish and Cook returned to the woods that night to get their tools they found that the tools had vanished. They spotted the smoke of a large fire in the distance.

The group decided to put plans in place to respond in the event of an attack. Miles Standish was officially elected their captain—a position he would hold for the next 40 years. He drew up a schedule for guard duties, and made it clear that they must, at all costs, disguise how many were currently sick or dying. When someone sounded the alarm signaling that there were Indians nearby, even those who were

Samoset was the first friendly Indian contact the Pilgrims had in the New World. The Abenaki provided the settlers with much valuable information.

very sick were pulled out of bed and propped up against a tree with a musket in their hands.

FRIENDLY CONTACT

The Pilgrims knew that they were building their homes on territory that had been cleared by Indians. What they did not know was how many were nearby, and whether or not they would return to claim their land.

To provide some additional defense in the event of another attack, Captain Standish advised them to bring the cannons from the *Mayflower*. There were two large iron cannons, as well as several smaller ones. These were hauled up the hill to the spot where a gun platform had been built.

In March the weather grew warmer. Standish had decided that the men in the settlement needed to meet regularly to discuss their defenses and plans for a military attack. On Friday, March 16, they were in the middle of one of these meetings when a tall, black-haired Indian appeared in the woods, carrying a bow and arrow. The Pilgrims reached for their muskets and watched in some astonishment as the Indian continued to walk toward them. He moved past the row of houses and walked right up to a group of men. To their amazement he said, "Welcome, Englishmen!"

In *Of Plymouth Plantation* Bradford notes that the Indian spoke "broken English, which they could well understand." He explained that he was not from this region, but instead had come from Pemaquid Point, near Mohegan Island on the coast of Maine, an area where English fishermen frequently came to fish. It was from them that he had learned English. His name, he said, was Samoset.

The Pilgrims gathered around to listen to him, somewhat distracted by the fact that he was practically naked, wearing only a fringed bit of leather around his waist. Finally, one of the Pilgrims draped a red coat over him, no doubt to enable them to better concentrate on what he was saying.

They asked him if he would like something to eat. He quickly requested beer, which they did not have, but instead they offered him biscuits, butter, cheese, pudding, and a slice of roasted duck, which he seemed to enjoy.

THE WAMPANOAG

When the Pilgrims first arrived in the area they named Plymouth, the region was part of the lands inhabited by Native Americans known as the Wampanoag. Archeological records reveal evidence of Wampanoag presence dating back some 5,000 years.

The Wampanoag are known as "the People of the Light" or "People of the Dawn." They lived throughout southeastern Massachusetts and parts of Rhode Island, particularly the region stretching from Narragansett Bay and the Pawtucket River to the coast of the Atlantic Ocean, including Martha's Vineyard and Nantucket. They moved between different sites, depending on the seasons, traveling to specific villages for planting, fishing, hunting, and harvesting.

At the time of the Plymouth settlement, there were approximately 30 Wampanoag villages in the region. The peace treaty signed with the Pilgrims by the Wampanoag chief Massasoit was critical to the success of the settlement, as was the Wampanoag's willingness to share their agricultural and hunting traditions, which enabled the Pilgrims to plant and harvest crops after their first winter.

The Wampanoag traded with the Pilgrims, and later helped them explore the surrounding areas. In 1621 the Pilgrims and Wampanoag celebrated the first Thanksgiving, marking a successful harvest and a first year of peaceful coexistence and cooperation.

There are still Wampanoag living in communities around Martha's Vineyard, Cape Cod, and the Narragansett Bay, including tribal communities at Mashpee and Aquinnah. Many Wampanoag words, introduced to the Pilgrims to explain the animals and plants that were new to them, are part of our language today. These include skunk, moose, squash, pumpkin, succotash, and moccasin.

He explained to them that the Indian name for the area where they had settled was "Patuxet," meaning little bay. The Patuxet Indians, who had once lived here clearing the land and planting corn, had nearly all been killed by a mysterious illness that swept through the region about three years earlier. Samoset only knew of one person who had survived, and he spoke even better English because he had spent time in England. His name was Squanto.

Samoset also explained that all of the Indians in the region were ruled over by a chief named Massasoit of the Wampanoag tribe. The Wampanoag lived about 40 miles (64.4 m) away in a place called Pokanoket. Squanto was also living in Pokanoket, Samoset explained.

Samoset spent the night in the settlement and was presented with gifts—a knife, a bracelet, and a ring—and asked to return with some of the Wampanoag and furs or any other items that they might be willing to trade with the Pilgrims.

Samoset returned five days later, bringing with him four other Indians, including Squanto. Bradford described Squanto not only as an interpreter but as "a special instrument sent of God for their good beyond their expectation." His helpfulness would gradually be revealed as an effort to cement his own power in the region. But his contribution to aiding the early negotiations between the Pilgrims and Indians and his instructions to the Pilgrims in "how to set their corn, where to take fish, and to procure other commodities," in Bradford's words, as well as his familiarity with the region, would prove invaluable to the success of the Plymouth colony. Other English colonies, whose initial contacts with Indians were hostile, did not benefit from the valuable guidance in which crops to plant and how to procure food for sustenance, and as a result they suffered periods of starvation.

In this first meeting, Squanto explained that the Indian leader Massasoit and his brother, Quadequina, were nearby and wished to meet with the Pilgrims. About an hour later Massasoit appeared on the hill. He was tall and imposing. His face was painted dark red, and he was wearing a large necklace made of white shells. He had a long knife hanging at his side. He was accompanied by 60 warriors, whose faces were painted black, red, yellow, or white. Some had furs draped over their shoulders. All had bows and arrows.

TREATY WITH MASSASOIT

One of the Pilgrims, Edward Winslow, was selected to go with Squanto to greet Massasoit. He put on his armor, draped a sword at his side, and went up the hill to present a pair of knives, some copper chains, some biscuits, and a jar of alcohol. The Indians ate the biscuits and drank the alcohol, then expressed an interest in Winslow's armor and sword, which he politely refused to give them. Winslow knew that the Pilgrims had barely 20 healthy men and he was surrounded by 60 warriors out of what was undoubtedly a far larger tribe. He expressed, on behalf of Governor Carver, the Pilgrims' interest in establishing trade and a formal peace. Eventually they agreed that Winslow would stay with Quadequina and most of the warriors, as a kind of hostage, while Massasoit and 20 of his warriors went to meet with Governor Carver.

Massasoit was formally conveyed by Captain Standish and six armed men to one of the houses, which was still under construction. A green rug and some cushions were placed on the dirt floor. A drum and trumpet played as the governor and a few other Pilgrims marched into the house.

The two leaders formally kissed each other's hand, and then sat on the green rug. The two drank what the Pilgrims described as "strong water" (alcohol) and then began to negotiate a peace treaty.

Bradford noted the six key terms of the treaty:

1. Neither Massasoit nor any of his people should injure or "do hurt" to any of the Pilgrims, nor should the Pilgrims injure any of the Wampanoag.

2. If any of Massasoit's people did injure any of the Pilgrims, the Indian would be sent to the settlement so that they might determine his punishment. The same would be true if the Pilgrims injured any Indians.

3. If anything were taken from the Pilgrims it would be returned, and the Pilgrims would do the same with the Indians' property.

4. If anyone did "unjustly war" against Massasoit's tribe, the Pilgrims would assist them; and if anyone attacked the Pilgrims, Massasoit would come to their aid.

5. Massasoit would notify his allies of the terms of this agreement, so that they would know not to attack the Pilgrims.

6. Whenever the two groups met, they would leave their weapons behind.

Once the terms were agreed upon, Massasoit left. But Squanto, it was agreed, would remain behind with the Pilgrims. Francis Dillon describes this meeting in *The Pilgrims* as the most important event in the life of the Plymouth settlement since the actual landing. The outcome would provide the means for the Pilgrims' security. The peace treaty would last more than 50 years, until 1675.

DEPARTURE OF THE *MAYFLOWER*

In spring, the sickness and death that had plagued the settlement finally came to an end. The crew of the *Mayflower* had been devastated by illness. In late March Master Jones was confident that the survivors had recovered sufficiently and could begin preparations for the journey back to England. It is important to note that, despite the hardships and illness they had already suffered, despite the fact that so many had lost loved ones, none of the Pilgrims chose to give

The peace treaty between Massasoit and Governor Carver assured the Pilgrims security for the next half-century.

up and sail with the *Mayflower* back to England. In fact, one of the crew—a cooper (barrel maker) named John Alden—decided to stay with the Pilgrims.

Originally the Pilgrims had intended to fill the hold with items for the Merchant Adventurers, such as timber, furs, and fish—a down payment on the amount they owed to their investors. But they had not yet traded enough furs or mastered the art of harvesting cod or other fish. Because of illness, they had not had time to cut down enough timber even to complete the building of their homes. Instead, stones were loaded into the hold of the ship for ballast. The *Mayflower* set sail on April 5.

The *Mayflower* arrived at the port of Rotherhithe, a short distance from London, on May 6, 1621. The return voyage had been far faster, less than half as long as the trip to New England.

The *Mayflower* made one final voyage. Master Jones and his ship sailed to France to convey a cargo of salt. Shortly after returning from France, Master Jones died and the ship lay idle in port, eventually rotting away.

A NEW SEASON

By April, fish began to swim through the waters around Plymouth, including two species of herring. Squanto showed the Pilgrims how to catch the fish and explained the role they played as fertilizer in the Indian system of planting. He demonstrated how to use the corn seed they had stolen several months earlier, planting it in mounds of earth along with several dead herring. When the corn sprouted, the Indians then planted squash and beans. The squash and beans sent out creeping vines, which attached to the cornstalks and provided shade from the sun while preventing weeds.

Squanto also explained when the planting should begin. According to *The Pilgrims* this was "when the leaves of the white oak were as large as a mouse's ear." The Pilgrims set aside 20 acres (8 hectares) for their first crops, and then followed Squanto's instructions about how to set traps for the herring.

Bradford notes that the Pilgrims followed Squanto's instructions carefully, while also planting some of the English seed they had brought with them—seed for wheat and peas. This "came to no good, either by the badness of the seed or lateness of the season or both, or some other defect."

The Pilgrims all worked together planting these crops. It was exhausting work—the heavy baskets of fish needed to be retrieved from the river and then carried to the fields. The crops had to be thinned, well hoed, and watched to ensure that the seed was not eaten by crows and wolves did not dig up the dead fish. On one warm April day, after working in the field, Governor Carver complained of a headache and went home to lie down. Within a few hours he had fallen into a coma. He never recovered, and died several days later.

Carver had been greatly respected by the Pilgrims and his death was a special blow, coming just as so many had recovered from illness and the hopeful acts of planting seed and harvesting fish had begun. His wife died about five weeks later. Unlike the secret burials that had taken place when they were striving to prevent the Indians from learning how many had been lost, Carver was buried with the finest honors they could give him. The men fired off their muskets as a gesture of honor.

It was critical to choose a new leader who could hold the settlement together, oversee continued negotiations with the Indians, and smooth over the differences that occurred among the settlers. They chose William Bradford. Because Bradford was still recovering from illness, Isaac Allerton was appointed his assistant.

Bradford was 31 years old when he became the governor of Plymouth. The fate of the new colony was largely dependent on the decisions he would make.

5

The First Thanksgiving

One of William Bradford's first official acts as governor was a joyful one. Edward Winslow and Susanna White, who had each lost spouses when illness swept through the settlement, decided to marry each other. On May 12 the first wedding in the Plymouth settlement was performed. It was a civil, rather than a religious, ceremony (the Pilgrims believed that nowhere in the Bible was it specified that weddings must be performed by ministers), and William Bradford officiated as the settlement's governor.

Bradford oversaw the continued construction of the settlement, as well as the planting and planning. Having suffered through one hard winter, the Pilgrims now knew what to expect from the weather and were determined to have plenty of food to last them through the next one. There was one worry in connection with the effort to hoard supplies. The Pilgrims had cemented their friendship with the Indians living in the region so effectively that they were being besieged by a steady stream of Indians dropping in and expecting some show of hospitality. If they provided food and drink to all of these unexpected guests, they would not have enough supplies to last them through the winter.

Bradford wisely decided to send two men to visit Massasoit and ask him to reduce the number of visitors to a more manageable select few. Edward Winslow and Stephen Hopkins were chosen for the mission, and were instructed to spend some time exploring the surrounding areas on their way to and from Massasoit. Squanto served as their guide.

It took them two days to travel the 40 miles (64.4 km) west to Massasoit's village. What was most apparent was the emptiness of the region—the Wampanoag had been devastated by the illnesses that swept through so much of the native population. "They not being able to bury one another, their skulls and bones were found in many places lying still above the ground where their houses and dwellings had been, a very sad spectacle to behold," Bradford notes. They also learned that another tribe—the Narragansett—lived across the bay and had been unaffected by the plagues that killed so many three years earlier. They now continually threatened the Wampanoag.

Winslow, Hopkins, and Squanto were treated well as they traveled toward Massasoit's village. They were offered food—corn bread, herring roe, boiled acorns, roasted crab, and shad—by the Indians they encountered along the way, until finally they reached the fertile land where Massasoit's village was situated.

They were ushered into Massasoit's wigwam and presented him with gifts, including a horseman's coat and a copper chain. The chain had a specific purpose; if there was a special guest that had been sent to the Pilgrims whom Massasoit wished them to entertain he was to give that guest the copper chain. If the Pilgrims saw the copper chain they would know that he had been sent by Massasoit and would share their food and drink with him. Others could be refused. Massasoit willingly accepted the gifts and agreed to the request.

Massasoit then began a long and tedious speech in which he recited the number of villages that paid him tribute and how he would encourage each one to trade furs with the Pilgrims. As each village was named, Massasoit's men recited several phrases confirming Massasoit's influence there and how the Pilgrims would benefit from peace and trade with that village. On and on the speech went, until more than 30 villages had been named, Massasoit's influence there was confirmed, and the pledge of peace and trade with that village made.

It was growing late, and the Pilgrims were becoming hungry, but no food was offered. Apparently Massasoit and his people had only recently arrived there as part of their seasonal migration, and had not yet had time to hunt or fish. Finally, hungry and tired, Winslow and Hopkins indicated that they wanted to sleep. Massasoit insisted that the guests be given the bed in his wigwam. It was actually more of a platform—a wooden plank raised about a foot off the ground with a thin mat on top. When Winslow and Hopkins accepted, they soon discovered that they would be sharing the bed with Massasoit, one of his wives, and two of Massasoit's warriors, all crowding in together.

The next day the Indians asked Winslow and Hopkins to demonstrate the accuracy of their muskets. By afternoon two large fish were produced and boiled, but with more than 40 people crowding around for a taste the portions were quite small. Winslow and Hopkins spent one more sleepless night in the same circumstances before deciding to leave, fearing that if they did not leave soon they would be too weak from hunger and lack of sleep to survive the return journey. Two days later they were back in Plymouth, reporting a successful mission and a better sense of the land to the west.

The first wedding in the Plymouth settlement took place on May 12, 1621, between Edward Winslow and Susanna White. Puritan weddings were civil rather than religious, and they were modest affairs, as depicted in this illustration.

OTHER ALLIES

A few weeks after Winslow and Hopkins returned from their diplomatic mission, a 16-year-old Pilgrim named John Billington wandered away from Plymouth to explore the woods south of the settlement and became lost. Billington's family had gained a reputation for being troublemakers. His younger brother, Francis, had nearly blown up the *Mayflower* several months earlier when he fired a musket on board, dangerously close to a barrel of gunpowder. His father had had several public feuds with Captain Miles Standish. And now John Billington was lost.

He spent several days wandering in the woods, surviving on berries and whatever else he found. Gradually, he made his way to an Indian village called Manomet, some 20 miles (32.2 km) south of Plymouth. From there, he was taken to the Nausets, who lived in Cape Cod. It was the Nausets who had attacked the Pilgrims when they first landed in Massachusetts in December. It was also the Nausets whose corn seed the Pilgrims had stolen.

Bradford sent out messengers to try to find John Billington and eventually word came from one of Massasoit's men that the young Billington was being held by the Nausets. Bradford now had several pieces of information to evaluate. One of these was that Massasoit had no influence over the Nausets; otherwise he would simply have asked for Billington to be returned to Plymouth. The other was that Billington was still alive. There was an opportunity for negotiation, but it had to be done carefully.

Bradford ordered 10 men (more than half the adult males in the settlement) to form a rescue party and head east by boat to the area controlled by the Nausets. Squanto and another Indian, Tokamahamon, went with the party to serve as guides and interpreters.

The Nausets were very numerous and the Pilgrims, when they reached the shores of Cape Cod, were quickly surrounded. One very old woman confronted them, weeping and explaining that the English explorer Thomas Hunt had captured three of her sons. Soon, they encountered the man whose corn had been stolen; they promised to reimburse him and invited him to visit the settlement for a proper accounting of what had been taken.

Aspinet, the leader of the Nausets, appeared, surrounded by more than a hundred warriors. One of them was carrying John Billington, who apparently was completely unharmed and was now wearing a necklace of shell beads. Billington was handed back and the Pilgrims presented a knife to Aspinet. Peace was declared.

SHOW OF FORCE

While the Pilgrims relied on diplomacy in these early encounters, Bradford was equally committed to demonstrating the Pilgrims' willingness to fight if needed. Soon after the successful recovery of John Billington, one of Massasoit's men, a Wampanoag named Hobomok, came running into the settlement. He reported that Squanto was probably dead. Squanto had been sent by Bradford to a village east of Massasoit's village to investigate rumors that an Indian leader named Corbitant was trying to create trouble for Massasoit and the Pilgrims. Corbitant was supposedly one of Massasoit's allies, but as Bradford notes he was "never any good friend to the English." Hobomok reported that he had seen one of Corbitant's men holding a knife to Squanto's chest and threatening to kill him in an effort to disrupt the alliance between the Pilgrims and Massasoit.

When Bradford learned of this he immediately called for a meeting of his advisors. As Bradford wrote, "if they should suffer their friends and messengers thus to be wronged, they should have none would cleave to them, or give them any intelligence, or do them service afterwards." They decided that Standish and 10 well-armed men would attack Corbitant's village that night. If Squanto had been killed, they planned to cut off Corbitant's head and bring it back to Plymouth. Hobomok agreed to go with them, to lead them to the place where Squanto had been seized and point out Corbitant.

They arrived at nightfall, in the rain. Hobomok pointed out Corbitant's wigwam and Standish and several of the men ran in, while others stood guard outside and fired off their muskets. There were screams and much confusion, until they finally learned that Corbitant had left the village that day and Squanto was alive and well. The

THANKSGIVING FACT AND FICTION

The Thanksgiving holiday Americans celebrate today is derived from the celebration held by the Pilgrims in 1621, as they harvested their first crops in their new homeland and prepared to mark their first year of survival at Plymouth. But the myths and traditions that have been created around the holiday have little in common with the real experiences of those early settlers.

First, the Pilgrims did not refer to their celebration as a "thanksgiving." Instead, it was a kind of harvest celebration; William Bradford described it as a time to "rejoice," while Edward Winslow, in a letter printed in *Mourt's Relation* describes it as a time of entertaining and feasting "after we had gathered the fruit of our labours."

Paintings meant to depict the first Thanksgiving often show Pilgrims seated around a long table, with white tablecloth and dishes bearing plates of food, perhaps with a few Indians in the background. In fact, there were twice as many Wampanoag as Pilgrims at the celebration. There were not enough tables and chairs for everyone. Meat would have been roasting on outdoor fires,

frightened villagers produced an offering of the best food they had. Three villagers who had been wounded in the confusion were taken back to Plymouth, where their wounds were tended to and they were sent home.

For several weeks, chiefs of many of the villages in the region began sending messengers or, in at least nine cases, traveling themselves to Plymouth to pledge their friendship to the Pilgrims and sign peace treaties with them. Even Corbitant sent word through Massasoit that he wished to make peace with the Pilgrims, although and many of those at the feast would have eaten while standing around the fire or sitting on the ground nearby. There was not a single, formal meal. Food was eaten over the course of three days, with different groups eating sometimes together and sometimes separately. Forks and spoons were not used; food would have been eaten with the fingers or speared with a knife.

The exact date of this first Thanksgiving is unknown, but it probably took place in late September or early October. It was not until 1863 that President Abraham Lincoln specified a national Thanksgiving Day to be celebrated on the last Thursday in November.

The traditional Thanksgiving celebration today includes roast turkey (which the Pilgrims did have) and cranberry sauce and pumpkin pie (which they did not). Ducks, geese, and turkey were plucked and then roasted over a fire. Corn was ground into a kind of oatmeal called *samp* or made into corn bread. The venison brought by the Wampanoag was roasted on spits over a fire. The first Thanksgiving menu also included fish—probably striped bass, bluefish, and cod—as well as cabbages, onions, and squash.

perhaps wisely, as Bradford wrote, he "was shy to come near them a long while after."

CELEBRATING THE HARVEST

Bradford and the other Pilgrims had much to be thankful for as autumn arrived and they began to harvest their first crop. They had survived a difficult journey across the ocean and a brutal winter that had cost the lives of many of their friends and loved ones. They had

To celebrate the harvest and as a peaceful gesture, the Pilgrims sat down with their Indian neighbors to a fall feast in 1621. Today, Americans honor the event with a holiday now called Thanksgiving.

built a new community with seven houses, a common house, and three storage structures for food and supplies, and had learned the necessary skills for survival in this new land. They had successfully negotiated peace treaties with the Indians who lived nearby.

It was a "small harvest" that first year, Bradford noted, with crops of corn, peas, barley, beans, and squash. Bradford ordered a hunting party of four men to go out and bring back some of the ducks and geese that were migrating south for the winter. In one day the four men killed enough fowl to feed the community for a week. The Pilgrims had stockpiled supplies of salted cod, bass, and fish. There were also wild turkeys.

It was probably sometime in late September or early October of 1621 that the first Thanksgiving took place. Nathaniel Philbrick in *Mayflower* notes that William Bradford decided that the time had come to "rejoice together . . . after a more special manner." The Pilgrims did not use the term "thanksgiving" to describe this celebration.

As the harvest celebration began, Massasoit and about 100 of his men (more than twice the population of Plymouth) appeared at the settlement. When he learned that the Pilgrims were celebrating, he sent out several of his warriors to kill deer, as venison was one of the Wampanoag's favorite meats. They quickly returned, bringing five freshly killed deer. The feasting lasted for three days, and was accompanied by shooting competitions and other games, singing, and dancing. It would become an annual tradition for the Pilgrims to celebrate their harvest, giving thanks for each year of survival in their new home.

With the harvest in, they began to prepare the seven homes and the common house for winter. This winter, they believed, would be very different from the last. They were now healthy and strong and, as Bradford noted, they "had all things in good plenty."

6

New Settlers Arrive

Almost a year after the Pilgrims' arrival in Plymouth William Bradford received a message from some of the Indians living in Cape Cod. A ship had sailed into Provincetown Harbor.

Bradford notes that the ship was "unexpected or looked for"—it was too soon, he felt, for it to be a supply ship from England, considering that the *Mayflower* had left them a mere eight months earlier. For several days, Bradford learned from the Indians, the ship remained near the tip of Cape Cod. Finally, at the end of November, it was spotted sailing for Plymouth Harbor. The colonists anxiously assembled, worrying that the ship might be an enemy craft from France, intent on establishing its own colony nearby.

But as the boat neared, they saw to their relief that it was, in fact, an English ship: the *Fortune*. When the

Mayflower had brought back word that the Pilgrims had survived the winter and devastating illness and were establishing a settlement north of Virginia, the Merchant Adventurers had decided to send a new ship (smaller than the Mayflower) with 35 passengers and, more importantly, a patent giving the Pilgrims the legal right to settle on the land they had chosen.

The 35 passengers were for the most part "Strangers," in Bradford's words—people who were not part of the original Separatist group from Holland. Many of them were young men who had made the journey seeking adventure and perhaps the kind of financial success they could not hope to achieve in England. With their arrival, the size of the Plymouth settlement doubled. There were now 66 men in the colony and 16 women.

The arrival of these new settlers presented Governor Bradford with an immediate problem: where would they stay? There were still only seven houses and now four common buildings. Bradford divided the group, putting as many of the single men as he could in the common buildings and then dividing the others among the seven houses where families and other members of the community were already living in crowded conditions.

Bradford also had to face a more challenging problem: the colony had stored in supplies for the winter based on half as many people as now would need to be fed. "There was not so much as biscuit-cake or any other victuals for them, neither had they any bedding but some sorry things they had in their cabins; nor pot, or pan to dress any meat in; nor overmany clothes," Bradford wrote. The new arrivals had come without any needed supplies, with only enough food to last them the journey and nothing for the winter months ahead. "The plantation was glad of this addition of strength," Bradford wrote, "but could have wished that many of them had been of better condition, and all of them better furnished with provisions."

In addition to the fact that their chief representative with the investors, Thomas Weston, had failed to send them any new provisions, the *Fortune* also brought a letter from him in which he scolded the Pilgrims for failing to send back any furs, wood, or fish with the *Mayflower*. "I know your weakness was the cause of it, and I believe more weakness of judgment than weakness of hands. A quarter of the time you spent in discoursing, arguing and consulting would have done much more," Weston wrote in a letter that the furious Bradford included in *Of Plymouth Plantation*. Weston also asked them to provide some sort of detailed accounting of how the investors' money had been spent, and urged them to make sure that the *Fortune* was loaded with goods for her return trip.

The *Fortune* remained for only 14 days. Although its arrival was unexpected, and they had not had time to prepare a large quantity of goods, Bradford and the other Pilgrims loaded the ship with what they could spare. They managed to assemble two large barrels stuffed with beaver and otter skins. They also loaded clapboards made of split oak (Nathaniel Philbrick in *The Mayflower* explains that these would have been much smaller than modern clapboards and would have been used to make barrels rather than side houses). The total value of this freight was estimated to be about £500, roughly half of the debt they owed to the Merchant Adventurers.

Robert Cushman, part of the original congregation at Leiden and one of the men who had negotiated the contract with the Merchant Adventurers, had come over on the *Fortune* (illness had prevented him from sailing on the *Mayflower*). It was Cushman who had brought Weston's letter to Bradford, as well as the new patent giving the Pilgrims legal right to settle in New England. He was charged with returning with the *Fortune*, ensuring the safe delivery of the cargo to the Adventurers. He also carried with him a terse response to Weston's letter from Bradford. According to George D. Langdon, Jr., in *Pilgrim*

Robert Cushman gives a sermon to the Pilgrims upon his arrival in 1621. Cushman delivered a manuscript detailing the Pilgrims' first year in Plymouth to a British publisher.

Colony, Bradford's letter warned the Adventurers that the addition of so many new people to feed, without any supplies to help in the effort, would inevitably bring famine to Plymouth. Cushman also took with him a manuscript account of the first year at Plymouth, written by Bradford and Edward Winslow. It would be published in England the following year under the title *Mourt's Relation*. Cushman left one thing behind at Plymouth—his 14-year-old son, Thomas. He asked William Bradford to take care of his son until his return.

The Pilgrims would later learn that the *Fortune* was captured when it entered the English Channel. French pirates seized the ship and directed it at gunpoint to a small port in France. The cargo of furs and clapboard—the cargo that would have cut the Pilgrims' debt to their investors in half—was seized. Anything of value on the ship—even the shoes of those onboard—was taken. One of the few items not seized by the pirates was the manuscript providing an accounting of that first year. The emptied *Fortune* and its passengers and crew eventually returned to London.

CHALLENGES TO THE COLONY

Not knowing the fate of the *Fortune*, Bradford began to make plans for those in Plymouth to survive the winter. He was confident that the cargo sent back to England would produce another ship that would bring provisions to ensure the success of the colony. This was not likely to happen until the spring, however. It was December and there were several months of winter to endure and far more people in the colony than had originally been anticipated.

Many of the newcomers were unaccustomed to daily life in the settlement. They were not used to the tight living quarters and meager diet that was now routine to those who were beginning their second year in the New World. While there were still wild turkey, duck, and geese to be hunted, there would be no more fish until spring. There was only water and a small amount of wine to drink. Because there were no cows or goats there was no milk, butter, or cheese. There was inevitably grumbling among the new arrivals. They were disappointed that the vast wealth and abundant fertile soil described by John Smith and others who had traveled in the New World had translated into so little for them to actually eat.

Bradford began the unpleasant task of tallying up all the food that had been set aside for the winter and then redistributing it among the newly increased number of settlers. He discovered that, even if the rations were cut in half from what had originally been planned, they had enough food to last only six months. "So they were presently put to half allowance, one as well as another," Bradford wrote, "which began to be hard, but they bore it patiently under hope of supply."

Soon after the *Fortune* left, the Narragansett tribe, perhaps having learned that the ship had brought more people but no more supplies, sent a messenger to Plymouth, carrying a bundle of arrows tied up in the skin of a rattlesnake. When Squanto saw this, he told the Pilgrims that this was a threat and a challenge.

Bradford had already made what he thought were successful efforts to negotiate a peace treaty with the Narragansett leader, Canonicus. Now he knew that he had to respond with confidence. He removed the arrows from the snakeskin and filled it instead with gunpowder and bullets, then sent it back to Canonicus as a sign that if they preferred war to peace, the Pilgrims would be ready. The message seemed to have worked; eventually the snakeskin, still full of gunpowder and bullets, was returned to Plymouth.

Bradford worried that, at some point, a simple symbol would not be enough. He and Captain Miles Standish agreed that Plymouth needed a better system of defense. They decided to build a wooden wall, high enough to surround the settlement, with gates that could be shut and locked. It would need to be about eight feet (2.4 m) high, and almost a mile (1.6 km) in circumference. It would run from the common house, up to the cannon platform on Fort Hill, and back down to the common house.

In addition to the strenuous work involved in simply ensuring their basic survival, the Pilgrims now had to undertake this challenging construction project. The winter was growing harsh and they

THE NARRAGANSETT INDIANS

While the Pilgrims were able to successfully negotiate peace agreements and trade arrangements with many of the native peoples living around them, the Narragansetts remained a threat throughout much of Plymouth's history as a colony. The Narragansetts had a reputation in New England as fierce warriors. Their largest territory was in present-day Rhode Island.

Historical evidence suggests that the Narragansetts descended from peoples who had lived in that part of New England for 30,000 years. The first European to encounter the Narragansetts was Giovanni da Verrazano, who described a large population of Narragansetts living around Narragansett Bay when he explored the region in 1524. Weaker tribes paid tribute to the Narragansetts in exchange for protection, particularly as more and more Europeans began moving into the region. By 1636 Roger Williams was negotiating with the Narragansett tribe to obtain the rights to land in present-day Providence, Rhode Island. Later, the Narragansetts would join with Massasoit's son, known as King Philip by the English settlers, to fight against settlers from Plymouth as well as the

were surviving on half-rations. As described in *Mayflower*, a fence of that length, with three protruding gates to serve as shooting platforms, would require them to cut down hundreds of trees, strip away the branches, and chop them to the proper length. They then had to lug the 10- to 12-feet-long (3–3.7-m-long) logs from the forest back to the settlement. Using picks and hoes they had to dig trenches or holes two to three feet (0.6 to 0.9 m) deep, and then sink the trunks into the frozen ground. The trunks needed to be placed very tightly together to prevent a gap wide enough for an enemy to slip through. It took them more than a month to finish.

Massachusetts Bay and Connecticut colonies to reclaim their land. Narragansetts were brutally murdered during the Great Swamp Massacre in this conflict, known as King Philip's War.

Narragansetts, like many of the native tribes in New England, moved depending on the season. In winter, up to 20 families would share a longhouse inland. In the summer months, they moved to the coastline, where each family made its own wigwam or *wetu*, a temporary shelter made of bark and lined with woven mats. The Narragansett's diet included clams, johnnycakes (a kind of pancake made from cornmeal), succotash (a blend of corn and lima beans), quahog (clam) chowder, corn chowder, and strawberries.

The arrival of great numbers of English settlers in the region depleted the traditional hunting lands of the Narragansett. In the late 1800s the United States seized much of the tribe's land and the Narragansett population dispersed.

Today there are approximately 2,400 men and women who are direct descendants of the Narragansett tribe. Many of them still live in Rhode Island.

During the time of construction, Bradford wrote of an event that he described as a humorous incident. In reality it must have represented yet another test of his leadership. The event illustrates the differences between the group that had first dreamed of a new home in Holland and the "Strangers" who had joined them.

It was December 25, 1622—Christmas Day. To the "Strangers," many of them current or former members of the Church of England, it was a religious holiday. But to the Pilgrims it was an ordinary workday, based on their belief that a celebration of Christmas was not mandated in the Bible, nor was December 25 necessarily the correct date of Christ's birth. When Bradford summoned all the settlers to begin work on the fence, the "Strangers"—the majority of those newly arrived on the *Fortune*—protested, saying (as Bradford noted) that it was "against their consciences to work on that day." Reluctantly Bradford agreed, and then led the rest of the settlers out to continue the backbreaking work of hewing trees and forcing the timber into the frozen ground.

When they returned at noon, Bradford and the Pilgrims discovered that the Strangers were playing games in the center of the settlement, games like stool-ball, a game with a ball and bat like the English game of cricket, in which a ball is batted from stool to stool. Bradford then seized the balls and bats and told them it was against *his* conscience for some to work while others played. If Christmas Day was a religious holiday for them, he said, then they should spend it praying quietly inside, not "gaming or reveling in the streets." It was yet another reminder to the new arrivals that they were not in England anymore, and that this New World was not what they had expected.

A FALSE RUMOR

By March, the weather was slowly growing warmer and there was a hint of spring in the air. Bradford, hopeful that the cargo-laden *Fortune* would inspire additional ships to be sent to Plymouth, decided that it was time to once again trade for furs. They had obtained beaver furs from the Massachusetts tribe the previous year, and promised to return again to trade. He ordered 10 men, including Miles Standish, to prepare the boat to sail north to the Massachusetts territory.

Just as they were preparing to depart, Bradford was informed by Hobomok, one of the Indian translators, of a plot between the Massachusetts and Narragansett tribes to attack Standish and the other men when they arrived to trade. According to Hobomok, the plot was masterminded by the Narrangansetts, who planned to raid Plymouth. Hobomok accused Squanto of participating in the plot.

The settlers in Plymouth were desperate for food. They needed to be able to trade with the Indians, not only for furs but also for corn and other necessities. Bradford also felt that there was some jealousy between Squanto and Hobomok, and he decided that they should proceed with the trading mission. Bradford relied heavily on Squanto. He also knew that a similar relationship had sprung up between Hobomok and Captain Miles Standish and he suspected that the two Indians might be competing for influence within the settlement. To help deal with the conflict between the two, Bradford decided that both Hobomok and Squanto would go with the Pilgrims on the trading expedition.

In early April the trading expedition left Plymouth, heading by boat for the Massachusetts territory. Before they had been gone long, an Indian who was known to be a friend of Squanto's ran into the settlement. His face was bloody and he came with a frightening message: the Narragansetts had teamed up with Massasoit and both tribes were coming to attack Plymouth.

Bradford had to try to make sense of these recent events. Hobomok had accused Squanto of treachery, and it did seem a strange coincidence that news of the imminent attack would come so soon after Plymouth's military leader, Standish, had left with some of his best men on a trading expedition. He quickly ordered that the cannons be fired, in the hope that Standish and the others might hear the signal and turn the boat back to Plymouth.

Fortunately, the boat had not gone far and Standish and the others heard the noise and returned. When they learned of what had happened, Hobomok angrily accused Squanto's friend of lying, insisting that if Massasoit had planned an attack on Plymouth he

(Hobomok) would know of it. Bradford quietly pulled Hobomok aside and asked him to send his wife to Massasoit's village on some manufactured errand. While there, she would not arouse suspicion and could determine whether or not Massasoit and the others were preparing to attack Plymouth. Hobomok's wife discovered that Massasoit was in the village and there were no plans to attack the Pilgrims. Massasoit quickly learned the reason for her visit and became furious at Squanto and the suggestion that he would break the peace treaty.

Bradford soon discovered that Squanto had "sought his own ends and played his own game," as he wrote in *Of Plymouth Plantation*. During the past months he had gone through the neighboring villages telling them that the Pilgrims kept a plague buried in the ground in their villages and were preparing to use it against the Indians. He told them that if they paid him enough tribute, he (as a trusted Pilgrim advisor) could persuade them not to use the plague against certain villages. He had spent the better part of the winter building relationships with the villages so that they would depend on him, not Massasoit, to be their mediator with the Pilgrims. The final step in his plan was to cause the Pilgrims to attack Massasoit. With Massasoit gone, Squanto could then be the leader in the region.

Massasoit now made it clear that he expected the Pilgrims to honor one of the original points of their peace treaty—that any who had caused injury to them would be turned over to them for punishment. As added incentive, Massasoit told the Pilgrims that he would give them a large quantity of beaver skins in exchange for Squanto's head.

Bradford was unwilling to turn Squanto over to what would most certainly be his death. He had helped the colony in many ways, and despite this clear evidence of plotting, Bradford was reluctant to

That the Pilgrims survived their first year in the settlement was thanks in large part to Squanto. Later, however, he compromised the Pilgrims' peace treaty with Massasoit in pursuit of his own power.

comply with the treaty. Finally, just as he was about to turn Squanto over to Massasoit's men, a boat was spotted heading for Plymouth. Bradford quickly said that he wouldn't turn Squanto over until he knew where the boat was from. Massasoit's men were furious and immediately left Plymouth.

UNWELCOME NEWS

The boat, Bradford soon learned, had come from England. It was a fishing boat hired by Thomas Weston, one of the Merchant Adventurers. Not only had Weston not sent supplies to Plymouth, but in the letter brought by the ship it quickly became clear to Bradford that Weston was no longer going to support them as an investor. Instead, he had obtained a patent for his own settlement at the lower end of Boston Bay, and asked those at Plymouth to share their food and shelter with the people on board until their leaders found an appropriate settlement location. There were seven men on the first ship and, Weston made clear in his letter, more would be coming.

"All this was but cold comfort to fill their hungry bellies," Bradford wrote. Nonetheless they did the best to share the meager portions they had with these new arrivals. Two more ships arrived in the summer, bringing 60 more men that Bradford was somehow expected to feed and house. Once again, the people at Plymouth took pity on the new arrivals and shared their meager food supplies and housing with them. Many were sick, and the Pilgrims nursed them back to health.

The new arrivals were mostly rowdy young men who were unprepared for the structure and demands of life in Plymouth. Bradford instructed them to join in the planting of corn and other crops, but as soon as shoots and young plants began to appear the new arrivals, pretending to weed and tend the crops, actually ate as much of them as they could. A letter on the final ship carried the news that the

Fortune had been robbed before it reached England. The Plymouth settlers were saddened to find that their hard work had all been in vain. Worse still, with the ships arriving only with men and no supplies, Bradford gradually realized that there would be no more supplies coming from England. His colony was on its own. If they did not find a way to feed themselves, they would starve.

7

A Growing Colony

A letter from some fishermen in Maine provided the colony with a warning and Bradford with a new solution to the problem of how to feed the people living in his colony. The letter told Bradford and those in Plymouth that a group of Indians had massacred nearly 400 English colonists at the Jamestown settlement in Virginia. The letter, written by the captain of an English fishing vessel (and quoted by Bradford in *Of Plymouth Plantation*), explained that he was informing them of this development "that the old rule which I learned when I went to school may be sufficient; that is, Happy is he whom other men's harms doth make to beware."

Bradford was grateful for the warning. He knew that Plymouth (with only a quarter of the number of settlers as were at Jamestown) was still vulnerable to attack, and decided that the settlement needed not only a wall but also a fort. It would be built on top of a hill, with a flat roof and structures on which their cannons could be mounted. Guards could be posted at the fort to survey the surrounding area and send out warnings in case of danger. They could also use the fort as a meeting house.

Bradford also knew that his settlers, skilled in farming, had proved woefully inadequate at fishing. Despite the abundance of cod, bluefish, and striped bass in the surrounding area, they were still starving. The friendly warning from the fishermen inspired him to send a boat, with Edward Winslow on board, to thank the captain for the warning and find out if he might be willing to sell or trade some of the fish and other food he had. The captain welcomed Winslow, and gave him as much as he could spare without accepting any payment, then gave him a letter of introduction to the other English ships in the area and asked them to do the same. Winslow's boat was fully loaded when he returned to Plymouth. Unfortunately, when Bradford did some calculating he realized that there was barely a quarter of a pound of food for each person until harvest time. Bradford decided that the food needed to be rationed, so each day the Plymouth colonists went to the storehouse to receive that day's portion; otherwise, Bradford noted, he feared that "had it been in their own custody, they would have ate it up and then starved."

A POOR HARVEST

Thanks to the thievery of the men who had been sent by Weston to set up a competing settlement, the harvest resulted in a very poor crop. There was only a small portion of Indian corn and a few other vegetables to tide them through the winter. Weston's men had left Plymouth and begun their own settlement at Wessagussett, some 22 miles (35.4 km) north of Plymouth (in the area today known as

Weymouth). Bradford decided that, to avoid starvation, he would need to send out an expedition to trade for food with the Indians. When the men at Wessagussett learned of this plan they pleaded to be included. They could even supply the ship.

The joint expedition set out from Plymouth in November, heading south of Cape Cod under the command of Captain Miles Standish. Standish immediately became ill with fever and the ship returned. Knowing that it was a critical mission, Bradford decided that he would go in Standish's place. Squanto would go with them, too, to serve as Bradford's interpreter.

They quickly encountered storms and dangerous shoals, finally putting in on the south shore of Cape Cod, near present-day Chatham. Bradford and Squanto went ashore, and over the course of several days of negotiation they were able to trade for eight barrels of corn and beans. Bradford then wanted to continue to head south, for more trading, but as they were about to leave Squanto became ill with fever and bleeding from the nose. He died within a few days.

There was little time to mourn the Indian who had helped them in their earliest days in Plymouth. Bradford continued south to territory controlled by the Massachusetts tribe, and managed to obtain some additional barrels of corn and beans. But Bradford also heard extensive complaints about the conduct of Weston's men still in Wessagussett, specifically that they were stealing the Indians' food and supplies. Bradford returned to Plymouth with the much-needed food and prepared to confront the Wessagussett settlers.

Despite the supplies Bradford had helped them obtain on the trading mission, the settlers at Wessagussett were in a desperate situation. Unlike the Pilgrims, they had focused first on building a fort and not on farming, and as a result had almost no food supplies to sustain them. While the area around Wessagussett had plentiful shellfish, including oysters, they were afraid to leave the safety of the settlement to venture to the shore, even to gather desperately needed food. They feared the Massachusetts Indians, whose village was right next to the settlement (in Plymouth roughly 15 miles (24.1 km) separated the Pilgrims and the nearest Indians). First, they stole from the Indians. Gradually, as they began to starve, Bradford learned that they were selling anything they could to the Indians for a cup of corn—their clothing, their bedding, even themselves into slavery in order to be fed. The Massachusetts mocked the settlers, scorning their weakness and inability to survive.

At the same time, word reached Bradford that Massasoit was dying. He sent Winslow, Hobomok, and another Englishman, John Hamden, to make the 40-mile (64.3-km) journey, equipped with some medicine that might ease Massasoit's suffering. As they traveled they encountered some Indians who told them that Massasoit had died, but when they reached his village they discovered that he was not dead but blind and weak and suffering from what was probably typhoid fever. Winslow gave him some fruit preserves and later made a broth for him, and after eating and drinking Massasoit began to recover. He pledged his firm loyalty to the Pilgrims for saving his life and ordered that a great feast be prepared for his friends. During the feast Massasoit took Hobomok aside and spoke to him at length.

The next day, as they were returning to Plymouth, Hobomok revealed what he had been told: Plymouth was in great danger. The Massachusetts had decided to attack Weston's men at Wessagussett. They had the support of at least seven other Indian villages. Knowing that those in Plymouth would be furious if Wessagussett was attacked, the Indians planned to attack both settlements simultaneously. Hobomok was warning the Pilgrims to attack the

DAILY LIFE FOR THE PILGRIMS AND WAMPANOAGS

While the Pilgrims and Wampanoags lived only 40 miles (64.3 km) apart, their daily life was quite different. The Pilgrims had built houses from timber modeled after those in England, with steep roofs and a main room with a fireplace that was used for living, eating, and sleeping. There was often a small area for sleeping or storage above the main room. The houses had thatched, or straw, roofs. Massasoit's tribe lived in wigwams or *wetus*, structures made from saplings bent into circular shapes. In the summer, the frame was covered with woven mats of grass. In winter, bark was used as a covering, because it was a better protection against the snow and icy winds. Inside the *wetu* the Wampanoag slept on woven mats, using animal skins as blankets in winter. There was a fire pit in the middle and a smoke-hole in the roof, which could be covered if the weather was bad. The Wampanoag moved with the seasons; in the spring they lived in cleared areas where they planted corn, squash, and beans. Often these were near streams or on the coast so that the Wampanoag could fish. In the winter they moved inland to forested areas that offered more protection from the snow and cold.

Pilgrims wore several layers of clothing, even in the summer heat. There were layers of undergarments, stockings tied with garters for both men and women, hats, and shoes. The clothing they made at the settlement was woven by hand and colored using dyes made from plants or animals. The Wampanoag wore far less clothing. Men wore only a loose deerskin cloth around their waist along with a small pouch for their food or supplies. They went barefoot or wore moccasins made of deerskin. Men and women wore jewelry made of stone, bone, or clam shells.

Both Wampanoag and Pilgrims spent much of their day doing basic chores necessary for their survival, including fetching water and chopping wood for fires. Pilgrims hunted duck and geese, and collected mussels from the rocks along the shore. Their typical diet included cornbread and hasty pudding (a kind of oatmeal cereal). They ate three meals a day; the noontime meal was the largest. The Wampanoag hunted and ate rabbit, squirrel, turkey, and deer. Whatever was hunted that day would generally be prepared in a meat stew. The Wampanoag were also skilled fishermen, and caught clams, cod, bluefish, herring, and whatever else was in season in the rivers and ocean nearby.

Pilgrim children were expected to help their parents planting and harvesting crops, chopping firewood, tending the cooking fire, and fetching water. There were no schools. Parents might teach their children to read or write (if they had those skills themselves), and all Pilgrim children were expected to memorize and recite Bible verses. Wampanoag boys were taught the skills of hunting with bow and arrow. They had to learn how to make their own arrows, including the difficult process of using animal tendons to attach feathers to the end of the arrow. Certain strong boys were also selected to be *pniesog*, or warrior counselors, after a series of physical challenges and tests of their spiritual powers. These boys were then expected to serve as role models to the younger children, demonstrating courage, wisdom, and strength. Wampanoag girls were expected to help care for the younger children and were taught housekeeping and farming skills—in Wampanoag communities the women were responsible for farming.

*Source: www.scholastic.com/scholastic_thanksgiving/daily_life/

Massachusetts immediately, before the other Indian tribes could join them and begin the attack. Winslow and the others hurried back to warn Bradford.

A VIOLENT ATTACK

Bradford convened a meeting to decide what should be done. They were not yet under attack and they had heard false rumors before. But this time they decided that, as the news had come directly from Massasoit and seemed supported by the disastrous actions of those at Wessagussett, the Pilgrims agreed to launch a surprise attack.

Miles Standish, Hobomok, and seven of the settlers prepared to sail to Wessagussett, pretending to be on a trading mission. They could warn the men there and proceed to attack the Massachusetts.

When they spoke with some of the men at Wessagussett, they were told that they had nothing to fear from the Indians; in fact, some of them were living with the Indians in their wigwams. Meanwhile, a Massachusetts Indian appeared carrying some furs to trade. Standish pretended great interest in the trade, but something about his manner must have warned the Indian. He hurried back to his village and, soon after, two large warriors—named Pecksuot and Wituwamat—walked up to Standish and made a bit of a production of flashing and sharpening their knives. Pecksuot, who was quite tall, looked down on the far shorter Standish with a scornful gaze and, according to *The Pilgrims*, said, "You may be a great Captain but you are a little man. I am not a great Chief yet I am a man of great strength and courage."

The next day, Standish invited Pecksuot and Wituwamat into one of the settlement houses and offered them a meal. The Indians were joined by Wituwamat's brother and several women; the Pilgrims had Standish and three other Pilgrims plus Hobomok in the small room.

With threats of impending attack, Miles Standish tricked some Massachu-setts warriors by inviting them to a meal and then slaughtering them. Relations between the Indians and the settlers in the area were never the same.

Once they were seated and began to eat, Standish grabbed Pecksuot's knife (which was on a string around his neck) and began to stab him with it. The other Pilgrims grabbed Wituwamat and his brother. Wituwamat and Pecksuot were killed and the brother was taken outside and hanged. There were only a few male warriors in the village and all that were found were killed. Standish brought Wituwamat's head back to Plymouth and stuck it on a spike at the fort. It remained there for several years.

The attack on the Massachusetts dramatically changed the situation in that part of New England. The settlers at Wessagussett chose to give up. They took their ship and sailed north to Maine, where they arranged transportation back to England on an English fishing ship. The Pilgrims found that they were no longer able to trade with ease with the Indians; fearing attack, many of the tribes that had once willingly produced corn and furs now could not be found. The Pilgrims found the Indian villages abandoned. But with the attack on the Massachusetts and the disappearance of many Indians, those that remained increasingly turned to Massasoit for leadership.

A NEW COURSE

In the spring of 1623, concerned that the difficulty of trade might again mean not enough food if the harvest was poor, Bradford decided to make a dramatic change in the Pilgrims' farming practices. Previously, the Pilgrims had all worked a common plot, banding together to manage a community farm. But that April, Bradford decided to assign individual plots of land to each household. The families would be allowed to keep whatever they grew, but each household would be responsible for ensuring that its members had enough to eat from their plot's harvest. The results were dramatic. Each family now worked far harder than they had

This is a re-creation of the village built by the settlers. By the summer of 1623, 180 people lived in the Plymouth colony.

before. For the first time women, and even children, went into the fields to plant the corn and tend their plot of land. Much more corn was planted than ever before. The decision would prove one of the most important made by Bradford as governor; the colonists never again starved.

Four ships arrived at Plymouth during the spring and summer of 1623, bringing a total of 87 new settlers. One of these was a widow named Alice Southworth, who arrived with her two sons, Constant and Thomas Southworth. Alice was from Wrington, near Bath in England; her late husband had come from the area around Scrooby, and the Southworths and Bradfords had known each other in Leiden. Bradford had apparently sent several letters to Alice, though none have survived. Only a few weeks after Alice Southworth arrived at Plymouth—on August 14, 1623—she and William Bradford were married in a joyful ceremony somewhat unusual for the Pilgrims. In honor of the fact that it was the governor who was marrying, Massasoit came for the celebration, with a black wolfskin draped over his shoulders. He was accompanied by one of his wives and 120 of his warriors. The marriage feast featured venison—roasted and in meat pies—fish, plums, grapes, and nuts. Massasoit brought the venison plus a wild turkey, and the Indians livened the ceremony with dancing.

William and Alice would eventually have three children of their own—William Junior (born in 1624), Mercy (born in 1627), and Joseph (born in 1630). The Bradford household also included four boys who had been left in Bradford's care—Thomas Cushman, Nathaniel Morton, Joseph Rogers, and William Latham. William Bradford's son John, from his first marriage, did not join his father until sometime in 1628 or 1629, when he was 11 years old.

In addition to settlers, the ships brought livestock—goats, pigs, chickens, cows, and horses. By this time the Plymouth settlement numbered approximately 180 people, divided among 32 houses.

Many of the newcomers had paid their own way to Plymouth, and because of this they were not, they felt, subject to all of the rules and regulations of the colony. Gradually, differences began to sharpen between those who had taken on the debt owed to the investors and had responsibility to repay it with furs, clapboard, and other goods, and those who had no such obligation and were free to work only for themselves. Many of the new settlers were not Separatists, but instead were members of the Church of England, and soon they had summoned their own minister, a man named John Lydford, to come to the colony. Lydford landed in March 1624, and at first seemed to be an asset to the community. He joined the Plymouth church and renounced his ties to the Church of England. Gradually, Lydford became involved with the newer settlers, who were upset at the strict control Bradford exercised over the colony and at the religious intolerance they felt the Pilgrims demonstrated to any who did not share their beliefs. Many of these men were troublemakers—one of them pulled a knife on Miles Standish and swore at him when Standish ordered him to do his share of guard duty at the fort. Lydford soon disappeared, and was seen in his home writing several letters, which were then taken to a boat that was in the harbor preparing to depart for England.

Bradford secretly rowed out to the boat, whose captain was one of his good friends. With the captain's help he searched the boat and found more than 20 letters from Lydford to the Merchant Adventurers, which charged Bradford with poor leadership and those at Plymouth with discrimination, waste, and bad management. Bradford returned to Plymouth and, after a short time, called Lydford before the men of the settlement and demanded an explanation for the letters. Lydford at first said that he was simply writing on behalf of others in the settlement, but no one admitted that they had asked him to write the letters. Eventually Lydford confessed and begged for forgiveness. It was granted, but when it was discovered, within two months, that Lydford was again writing letters containing the same criticisms he was banished from Plymouth.

One of the consequences of the incident with Lydford was the breakup of the Merchant Adventurers, who had continuously been disappointed at the small return on their investment at Plymouth. Bradford and seven of the other men at Plymouth (including Edward Winslow and Miles Standish) agreed to buy out their shares in the colony, at a cost of £1800 (approximately $360,000 in today's dollars). They did not have this kind of money available, but took a loan which they attempted to pay back with shipments of furs and other goods. Neither Bradford nor the other Pilgrims were

astute financial managers, and there were ongoing troubles pay-
ing off this loan. Nathaniel Philbrick's *Mayflower* notes that Bradford calculated that between 1631 and 1636 the Pilgrims shipped
roughly £10,000 worth of beaver and otter furs (or about $2 million
in today's currency), but their debt never seemed to reduce. It was
a "great adventure," as Bradford noted, since they had "many other
heavy burthens [sic] already upon them, and all things in an uncertain condition."

8

The Great Migration

From 1630 to 1640 approximately 21,000 Puritan immigrants arrived in New England. Religious intolerance in England prompted their arrival, and now there was not only Plymouth but several other English colonies to the north, south, and west. In 1628 Plymouth had contained more English settlers than the rest of New England combined; two years later it could not even claim to be the largest Puritan colony. The leading Puritan colony was now the Massachusetts Bay Colony, which had begun with a few small settlements around the area now known as Boston, 30 miles (48.3 km) north of Plymouth. The largest of these was at Salem; in 1628 there were about 300 people living there, and another 100 living at a settlement known as Charlestown. In 1630 alone, 17 ships arrived from England bringing 1,000 settlers, most of whom worked to establish the Massachusetts Bay Colony.

Alden T. Vaughan in *New England Frontier* explains the significance for Plymouth of this wave of immigration: by 1632 the English population of the Massachusetts Bay Colony totaled 2,000; it doubled in the next two years. By 1637 there were close to 8,000 English settlers there. Plymouth, by contrast, had only 600 settlers.

Initially, this so-called great migration was helpful to the Pilgrims. The new settlers needed supplies and livestock until they were better established. The Pilgrims had livestock, particularly cattle and pigs, in excess, and could sell many to the newly arrived immigrants. They traded with the Dutch, who were setting up a colony to the south called New Amsterdam (which we now know as New York). The Pilgrims had also set up trading posts extending into present-day Maine and Connecticut. But gradually the settlers at Massachusetts Bay set up their own, competing trading posts.

Bradford was troubled by the departure from Plymouth of several of the families who had helped settle the colony. Even some of his close friends, such as Edward Winslow and Miles Standish, left seeking more and better land. Many of them moved across Plymouth Bay to a settlement that they named Duxbury. At first, those in Duxbury were expected to remain part of Plymouth and to return on Sunday to worship and participate in the responsibilities of the colony. By 1632 it was reluctantly agreed that they could formally leave Plymouth and set up their own community at Duxbury. Bradford seemed to feel this personally. In *Of Plymouth Plantation* he complained of the man who could no longer live "except he had cattle and a great deal of ground to keep them," and mourned the fact that "the town in which they lived compactly till now was left very thin and in a short time almost desolate. . . . I fear this will be the ruin of New England," he wrote. Even Bradford's oldest son, John, drifted away from the community, eventually settling in what is now Norwich, Connecticut.

HEAVY RESPONSIBILITIES

Plymouth was gradually being left behind as other colonies became the center of immigration and English settlement in New England. Bradford's responsibilities remained heavy, perhaps heavier as the fate of the colony seemed to suffer. He was responsible for overseeing the colony's trading efforts with the Dutch, with other English settlers, and with the Indians. In the event of disputes with any neighboring colonies, Bradford was called upon to serve as judge or negotiator on Plymouth's behalf.

Bradford worried about the spiritual component of Plymouth, particularly as the members of the original congregation at Leiden died or left the colony. He warned the other leaders at Plymouth that if serious steps were not taken to correct what he viewed as the growth of "wickedness," he would resign as governor. While the colony did recommit itself to a stronger spiritual component to daily life, the children of the original settlers lacked the passion and conviction that had characterized those who built the first homes at Plymouth.

Bradford was also alarmed at the decision of settlers from other colonies to provide the Indians with guns in exchange for food and other goods. He feared that these new settlers, accustomed to the peaceful coexistence he had worked so hard to achieve in the region, were too complacent in their dealing with the native peoples and would be unprepared for a conflict if one should arise.

In 1650 Bradford ended the journal that became *Of Plymouth Plantation*, noting that Edward Winslow had left the area four years earlier for England. Winslow never returned; he died in 1655 while on an expedition to the West Indies. Miles Standish died one year later, buried in Duxbury, the new community that he had helped to found. The final pages in *Of Plymouth Plantation* contain a list

Of plimoth plantation

And first of y occasion, and Indusments ther vnto; the which that y may truly vnfould, y must begine at y very roote & rise of y same. The which y shall endevor to manefest in a plaine stile; with singuler regard vnto y simple trueth in all things, at least as near as my slender judgmente can attaine the same.

1 Chapter

It is well knowne vnto y godly, and judicious, how ever since y first breaking out of y lighte of y gospell, in our Honourable nation of England (which was y first of nations, whom y Lord adorned ther with, after y grosse darknes of popery which had covered, & overspred y Christian world) what warrs, & oppositions ever since satan hath raised, maintained, and continued against the sainctes, from time, to time, in one sorte, or other. Some times by bloody death & cruell torments, other whiles Imprisonments, banishments, & other hard vsages. As being loath his kingdom should goe downe, the trueth prevaile; and y Churches of God reverte to their anciente puritie, and recover, their primative order, libertie, & bewtie. But when he could not prevaile by these means, against the maine trueths of y gospell, but that they began to take rooting in many places; being watred with y blood of y martires, and blesed from heaven with a gracious encrease. He then begane to take him to his anciente strategemes, vsed of old against the first Christians. That when by y bloody, & barbarous persecutions of y Heathen Emperours, he could not stoppe, & subverte the course of y gospell; but that it speedily overspred, with a wounderfull celeritie, the then best known parts of y world. He then begane to sow errours, heresies, and wounderfull dissentions amongst y professours them selues (working vpon their

The first page of William Bradford's manuscript, *Of Plymouth Plantation*, taken from his journals during the first years of Plymouth settlement. According to Pilgrim Hall Museum, "the Bradford journal is the single most complete authority for the story of the Pilgrims and the early years of the Colony they founded."

of the passengers who first sailed to Plymouth on board the *May-flower* with notes of what became of each of them.

In his final months of life, Bradford undertook a new challenge: he decided to learn Hebrew. Nathaniel Philbrick writes that this was part of Bradford's desire to perfect his study of the Bible. His health began to decline in the early part of 1657, and he died on May 9. He was 68 years old, and had been elected governor of the Plymouth Colony 30 times since 1621.

BRADFORD'S LEGACY

William Bradford, as the governor of Plymouth for most of its earliest history, inevitably stamped the colony with his personality, his beliefs, and his ideas. Bradford, through his emphasis on strong diplomacy and his willingness to adapt to Indian methods of cultivation and the use of Indian crops, set the tone for the early relationships built with the people native to the surrounding areas. His emphasis on strict rules for working, and the early focus on building a community through joint labor, sustained Plymouth through its earliest years and in large part ensured the colony's survival.

His writings, particularly *Of Plymouth Plantation*, provide a key record of the Pilgrims' history from their beginnings in Scrooby to the community in Holland, their journey on board the *Mayflower*, and the early years of the settlement. Far more than a simple historical record, *Of Plymouth Plantation* offers a more personal, often emotional account of the experiences of building a colony in a strange land.

The colony at Plymouth was frequently intolerant of those with differing religious beliefs, particularly the members of the Church of England and, later, the Quakers who joined the community. Because Bradford was governor, he must bear the responsibility

WILLIAM BRADFORD'S JOURNAL

William Bradford's journal, published under the title *Of Plymouth Plantation*, was written from 1630 to 1647. The journal is a history of the first 30 years of the Pilgrim colony at Plymouth and the only definitive history of the Pilgrims and the first years of the colony they founded.

The journal tells of the beginnings of the Separatist church in Holland in 1608 and the voyage on board the *Mayflower*. It details the selection of the site at Plymouth, the building of the colony, and its history until 1647.

Bradford was not an impartial witness. He was one of the leaders of the colony, and the journal offers his perspective on events and people. As governor of the colony for more than 30 years, Bradford was involved in the key decisions that shaped Plymouth and affected its growth.

The journal was written on a rag-based paper, which is far more durable than the wood-pulp-based paper we use today. There are 270 pages in the original journal, numbered by Bradford (with occasional mistakes in the numbering). The pages and ink have faded slightly and become discolored, but are still completely legible.

In the seventeenth and eighteenth centuries colonial historians consulted the Bradford manuscript for information about Plymouth. In the 1760s the manuscript was in Boston's Old South Church Library before disappearing for nearly a century. In the 1850s it was discovered in the library of the Bishop of London. It was finally returned to the United States at the end of the nineteenth century, and is currently at the State House in Boston.

*Source: www.pilgrimhall.org

for an atmosphere of intolerance that, in certain ways, mimicked the religious intolerance that had prompted the Separatists to leave England in the first place.

Samuel Morison, writing in his introduction to the 1952 edition of Bradford's book, describes it as "a story of a simple people inspired by an ardent faith to a dauntless courage in danger, a resourcefulness in dealing with new problems, and impregnable fortitude in adversity that exalts and heartens one in an age of uncertainty, when courage falters and faith grows dim." Cotton Mather, in *Magnalia Christi Americana: Or the Ecclesiastical History of New-England* (published in 1702), describes Bradford as "a person for study as well as action," who, upon his death, was "lamented by all the colonies of New-England as a common blessing and father to them all." "Men are but flocks," Mather wrote, "Bradford beheld their need. And long did them at once both rule and feed."

The Pilgrims were unlucky in choosing to settle at Plymouth. There was no harbor deep enough to accommodate larger ships and no river nearby. The land had already been heavily farmed by Indians. The colony did not have access to the oysters or lobsters plentiful in other coastal areas in the region. If they had been able to explore more extensively, or at least to more carefully consult the map they had purchased from John Smith, they might have decided to settle instead in the more easily navigable area that is now Boston. It was Boston that became the major port in New England, and the Massachusetts Bay Colony located there became the more powerful and populated colony.

But the Pilgrims had the good fortune of a wise and strong leader in William Bradford. The signing of the Mayflower Compact before they even began construction of their settlement established that Plymouth would be a colony based on laws. Their focus was not to get rich or find gold. They wanted to build a new home, a new

Under this stone
rest the ashes of
WILL^M BRADFORD
a zealous puritan &
sincere christian
Gov. of Ply. Col. from
April 1621 to 1657.
(the year he died
aged 69)
except 5 yrs.
which he declined.

William Bradford died on May 9, 1657. The longtime governor of Plymouth was buried on Burial Hill in Plymouth, where his grave remains.

community in a new land, where they could enjoy the kind of freedom they had never before experienced.

Bradford understood the significance of what he and his fellow Pilgrims were attempting. "As one small candle may light a thousand," he wrote, "so the light here kindled hath shone to many, yea in some sort to our whole nation."

Chronology

1590   William Bradford is born in Austerfield, England.

1602   Bradford begins to attend Separatist meetings in Scrooby, England.

1609   Bradford moves with the Scrooby Separatists to Holland.

TIMELINE

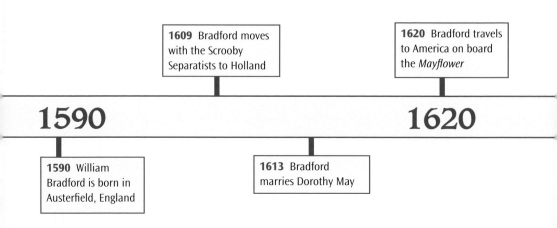

1609 Bradford moves with the Scrooby Separatists to Holland

1620 Bradford travels to America on board the *Mayflower*

1590

1620

1590 William Bradford is born in Austerfield, England

1613 Bradford marries Dorothy May

1613	Bradford marries Dorothy May.
1620	Bradford travels to America on board the *Mayflower*; Dorothy dies shortly after their arrival in December; the *Mayflower Compact* is signed; the settlement at Plymouth is founded.
1621	Plymouth's governor, John Carver, dies and Bradford is elected governor.
1623	Bradford marries Alice Southworth.
1630	Bradford begins the journal that will become *Of Plymouth Plantation*.
1650	*Of Plymouth Plantation* is completed.
1656	Bradford completes his final term as governor.
1657	William Bradford dies on May 9.

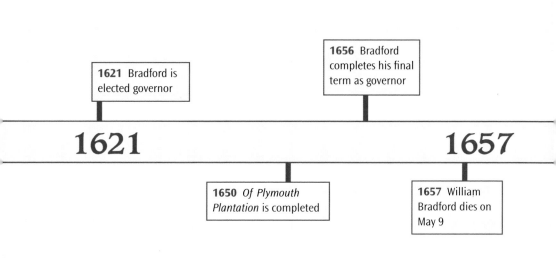

1621 Bradford is elected governor

1656 Bradford completes his final term as governor

1621

1657

1650 *Of Plymouth Plantation* is completed

1657 William Bradford dies on May 9

Bibliography

BOOKS

Bradford, William. *Bradford's History of Plimouth Plantation*. Boston: Wright & Potter Printing Co., 1901.

Bradford, William. *Bradford's History of the Plymouth Settlement: 1608–1650*. New York: E.P. Dutton, 1920.

Bradford, William. *Of Plymouth Plantation, 1620–1647*. New York: Alfred A. Knopf, 1952.

Bremer, Francis J. *The Puritan Experiment: New England Society from Bradford to Edwards*. New York: St. Martin's Press, 1976.

Deetz, James, and Deetz, Patricia Scott. *The Times of Their Lives: Life, Love, and Death in Plymouth Colony*. New York: W.H. Freeman, 2000.

Dillon, Francis. *The Pilgrims*. New York: Doubleday & Co., 1975.

Dow, George Francis. *Every Day Life in the Massachusetts Bay Colony*. New York: Benjamin Blom, 1967.

Hutchinson, Thomas. *The History of the Colony and Province of Massachusetts-Bay*. Cambridge, Mass.: Harvard University Press, 1936.

Langdon, George D., Jr. *Pilgrim Colony: A History of New Plymouth, 1620–1691*. New Haven, Conn.: Yale University Press, 1966.

Philbrick, Nathaniel. *Mayflower: A Story of Courage, Community, and War*. New York: Viking, 2006.

Rhys, Ernest, ed. *Chronicles of the Pilgrim Fathers*. New York: E.P. Dutton, 1910.

Taylor, Alan. *American Colonies: The Settling of North America*. New York: Penguin, 2001.

Vaughan, Alden T. *New England Frontier: Puritans and Indians, 1620–1675*. Boston: Little, Brown, 1965.

WEB SITES

Avalon Project—Mayflower Compact : 1620." Avalon Project—Documents in Law, History and Diplomacy. http://avalon.law.yale.edu/17th_century/mayflower.asp (accessed August 12, 2010).

"BBC—History." British Broadcasting Company (BBC). http://www.bbc.co.uk/history/ (accessed August 12, 2010).

Deetz, Patricia Scott , Christopher Fennell, and J. Eric Deetz. "The Plymouth Colony Archive Project." Historical Archaeology and Public Engagement. http://www.histarch.uiuc.edu/plymouth/ (accessed August 12, 2010).

"Henry Wadsworth Longfellow." Maine Historical Society. http://www.hwlongfellow.org (accessed August 12, 2010).

"Historical Perspective of the Narragansett Indian Tribe." Narragansett Indian Tribe. http://www.narragansett-tribe.org/history.html (accessed August 12, 2010).

"History and Culture." Mashpee Wampanoag Tribe. www.mashpee-wampanoagtribe.com (accessed August 12, 2010).

Preservation Virginia. "History of Jamestown." Jamestown Rediscovery. http://www.preservationvirginia.org/rediscovery/page.php?page_id=6 (accessed August 12, 2010).

Johnson, Caleb . "Caleb Johnson's Mayflower History." MayflowerHistory.com. http://www.mayflowerhistory.com (accessed August 12, 2010).

Kelso, Dorothy Honiss . "William Bradford." The Pilgrim Society. http://www.pilgrimhall.org/bradfordwilliam.htm (accessed August 12, 2010).

"Monarchs of Britain." Britannia: British History and Travel. http://www.britannia.com/history/monarchs/ (accessed August 12, 2010).

"The Wampanoag: People of the First Light." Boston Children's Museum. http://www.bostonkids.org/educators/wampanoag/ (accessed August 12, 2010).

Further Resources

BOOKS

Grace, Catherine O'Neill. *1621: A New Look at Thanksgiving*. Washington, DC: National Geographic Children's Books, 2004.

Hurst, Carol Otis, and Otis, Rebecca. *A Killing in Plymouth Colony*. Boston: Houghton Mifflin, 2003.

Lukes, Bonnie L. *Colonial America*. San Diego: Lucent Books, 2000.

Peters, Russell. *Clambake: A Wampanoag Tradition*. Minneapolis, MN: Lerner Publications, 1992.

Philbrick, Nathaniel. *The Mayflower and the Pilgrims' New World*. New York: Putnam, 2008.

Rinaldi, Ann. *The Journal of Jasper Jonathan Pierce: A Pilgrim Boy*. New York: Scholastic, 2000.

Tracy, Kathleen. *Plymouth Colony: The Pilgrims Settle in New England*. Hockessin, DE: Mitchell Lane Publishers, 2007.

WEB SITES

Mashpee Wampanoag Tribe
www.mashpeewampanoagtribe.com

Native Languages of the Americas
www.native-languages.org/wampanoag.htm

PBS's Freedom: A History of US
www.pbs.org/wnet/historyofus/web03/segment1.html

Pilgrim Hall Museum
www.pilgrimhall.org

Plimouth Plantation
www.plimouth.org

The Plymouth Colony Archive Project
www.histarch.uiuc.edu/plymouth/index2.html

Scholastic's The First Thanksgiving
www.scholastic.com/scholastic_thanksgiving

Picture Credits

PAGE

Index

Page numbers in *italics* indicate photos or illustrations. Page numbers followed by *m* indicate maps.

About the Author

Heather Lehr Wagner is a writer and editor. She is the author of numerous books exploring political and social issues, including several books focusing on the people who shaped colonial America. She is also the author of *Benjamin Banneker* in the LEADERS OF THE COLONIAL ERA series.

Heather Lehr Wagner earned a B.A. in political science from Duke University and an M.A. in government from the College of William and Mary. She lives with her family in Pennsylvania.